dear cloud

dear cloud

letters home from a
long distance traveler

marc peter keane

marc peter keane • mpk books
isbn: 978-0615425344
cover image is of the omega nebula from esa/hubble

tide pool

dear cloud

i have been a tide pool on a rocky shore, a cleft in a mile-long outcropping of basalt that catches water like an upturned leaf. just a thimble from the bucket of the bay.

each morning salt waters flow into me, shivered in by lapping waves that quiver and hiss as they fill me with small presents. sand and pebbles that tumble in with their tiny scrapings. shards of glass, some glinting, sunlit, most dull-ground and mute. shreds of rope, broken pieces of shell, a shattered piece of bright buoy. sand dollars wash in with urchins, bobbing moonjellies, schools of young sculpins, and billions of smaller lifesparks, some plant some animal, smidgens of existence that fill the water with suggestions of bigger things to be. the salt water and its bounty fill me and then cover me until i am no more, erased beneath the waves, just one more dent on the coastal floor.

then come the quiet hours, high tide, subsumed by water, the rolling pull of the waves above me but a distant presence. all the rockweed and nailbrush that grow along my edges float up in frilly curtains and sway softly through beams of angled sunlight. gangs of spiked urchins nibble their way across my hollow, scouring their paths of plant life. the clustered mouths of barnacles open and close in quick gulps as they shoot out appendages that look like fanned tongues or lacy hands grasping at the water, tugging in what miniscule bits of food they chance to find. nearby, anemone rest patiently, anchored to small cracks, waiting for fish to nestle into their fronds. fish seeking shelter, finding something else entirely. once a crab was grabbed by a large anemone. as it was drawn inside, its armored body enfolding deep into the pulsing muscle, it slowly disappeared from sight until only one red claw remained hanging outside, waving back and forth, as if beckoning.

come here, come here. you gotta see this.

or, maybe, just to say goodbye.

after a few hours the tide turns, the irresistible tug slides into reverse, and the salty waters are sucked from me back into the bay along with anything that isn't tied down. the barnacles stay, as do the anemone and the seaweed

— my constant friends — but the rest washes out to sea and on to parts unknown. if it's daytime, i lie exposed to the sun, drying. in summer baking, the dark basalt as hot as a griddle. what has legs scurries for cover in cracks and crevices, down into the puddles of water such as remain in my deepest parts. what can't move languishes under the sun, cooking. at night, i lie open to the stars searching through that other ocean. i count them and think of home. and you.

then the surge turns yet again, sending new waters flooding over me. all this, twice a day, every day, without fail. in and out, like breathing.

when it rains, clear water runs in fine rivulets off the stone outcroppings, finding its way down across the rocky shore, pouring into me in cool streams. it tastes sweet at first and later, if the rains continue hard and strong, it carries in bits of the forest that grows beyond the shore, fallen leaves and twigs and parts of many small bodies, the vinegary taste of decay.

most days, visitors come from above to look into me. flocks of gulls strut about squawking, poking through the water with their splayed bony feet, pecking incessantly at everything from seaweed to seashells. an otter slips into my pool, a sleek squeeze of fluid muscle, bobbing and diving, over and over. it picks up a smooth stone and an urchin from the bottom and returns to the surface. floating on

11

its back, it lays the stone on its belly, uses it to smash the urchin open, feasts, then rolls and dives for more. by the time it leaves, the pool is a thin soup of entrails and black spines. the crabs had a field day.

a boy came one day and stood peering into my shallows, tentatively jabbing his spear at things he saw. he looked deeper and deeper into the water, searching in hidden places for a movement or a color that would betray hiding prey. he was very quiet as he squatted there looking, black eyes in his sunbrowned face fixed intently on the bottom of the pool. eyes like pools themselves. as he looked, rafts of bubbles from the surf were nudged across the surface by the breeze, gathering where he crouched ankle-deep in the water. hundreds of bubbles, shiny and clear, skinned with undulating patterns of green and purple, passed across the surface in front of him. his focus shifted from the bottom of the pool to those colored isles and he noticed that in each bubble, he could see the reflection of the entire sky. the deep, deep blue dome, the long, striated clouds, and the flocks of gulls circling high above. and then, he saw himself. no, hundreds of himselves, wide-eyed, staring back up from all those iridescent domes. the realization came on him like warm air that spread as a grin across his face, ear to ear. seeing *that* made him smile even more.

an octopus came skulking into me and poked around a small cave-like overhang for some time. she liked the place well enough to lay her eggs and stayed on to guard them, spitting ink at the slightest provocation. sea slugs have left their spaghetti-filled sacs with millions of beaded off-spring. sculpins deposited maroon clusters of eggs in the hollows of mussel beds. when these broods hatch there's a sudden flurry of activity. little midges swimming in a panic everywhere and everything else showing up to eat.

the ocean is a huge thing, and i was no more than a teardrop, yet in all these comings and goings, the living and the dying, the solid parts and those fluid, i held within me a universe.

i was a pool of death   a pool of life
i was nothing if not restless

the fire within

dear cloud

i have been an ancient cedar, filled with light.

in a range of high-peaked mountains that rose in steep ranks from the shore, at a place within, where the warm, moist ocean air flowing in each morning met cold air sinking down from the highest reaches, heavy mists would form and whorl in a confusion of eddies, spinning up and around all the boulders and gravel slides that lay strewn down the precarious slopes. watered by those mists, a stand of massive cedars grew. silent, dark. thick trunks reaching up impossibly high into the air, their shattered branches spreading out in all directions like some arcane botanical rigging set out to trawl moisture from the air.

the years counted within their trunks in alternating rings of hard and soft rose near a thousand. i merged with one particularly tall tree that stood off to the side on a bluff overlooking the valley.

each day the mists left me freckled with small pearls of water that would glitter in the sunlight when the clouds cleared. grey squirrels would make the long climb to my lower branches to frolic and mate and nest. ferns grew in the crotches of my branches in the upper reaches, mounds of fine moss filling in beneath them, small worlds of green with smaller yet within, like forests within forests within forests. eagles perched on the highest spire surveying everything that could be seen — the forest, the valley, the sea. water from the gravelly soil wicked up through me from root to trunk to needle rising hundreds of feet, woody cell to woody cell, seeping out at the top as invisible breath. the unforgiving sun traced its heat over me in summer. in winter bitter winds left me glittering inside thin scanes of ice.

my days passed this way. the touch of the mist and small animals. the heat and the cold. the wind yanking at me from the sea. the constant ebb and flow of water through my inner skin.

this morning was hot, strangely hot, the air all full of darts and sudden changes. at the horizon, heavy clouds had formed and were approaching with wonderful speed, a heady rush of thunderheads like dark horses on the move. what a thrill to be there before them, the air chilling and dropping in surprise.

the wind picked up, scuffling through the forest, combing through our canopies and snatching out our deadwood, sucking all the moisture off our needles before the clouds opened and soaked us anew. thunder drummed distantly, first high then low, right and left, occurring and echoing all at once. i could feel the wind beginning to bend me, rock me side to side, my roots lifting lightly in the thin soil, tugging in the deep crevices where they held fast. the wildness of the day was pure rapture and i was filled to intoxication. blow, blow, break and burn and make me new.

lightning cracked across the valley. and then once more close by.

the third strike was me.

it was over in a moment. a blink, a gasp. but as i remember it now, i could feel it first in my roots, like electric water flowing up through my bark, wicking up through me from the ground toward a magnetic sky. it crackled as it rose, pulled up through me by that irresistible force above, from thicker trunk to thin, and then up that final naked spire that rose above my crown. what flowed through me, flowed from me. an ionized stream trickling out into the air on invisible threads of dust and moisture, leaping from point to point toward its muscular twin that stretched jagged down to meet it from the clouds above. and when those two streams reached each other, with their final co-ital touch, they released into each other an instantaneous birth of light and fire.

lightning. it's not like being struck. like being hit from above. it's you, *you*, yourself that is alive with this power. it flows through your skin and fills you from within and for the instant that it is growing inside you, your world is bright and sharp and filled with a tension that knows no bounds. you feel suddenly all undone, your matter sliding into energy, the stay-ties of solidity snapped, and you live for that immense instant in a dissolved state on the brink of elemental collapse.

i stood there on that bluff for so many years in all my majesty and yet everything of importance that happened to me, happened on my skin, flowing over and around me.

for all my girth
    i was but a passage for lighter things

wind child

dear cloud

i have been a girl on an endless plain filled to overflowing with light and wind.

we had a rough house of board and sod and an open
shed for the sheep to stand behind when the wind picked
up, blowing chaff and dust longways across the land, or
icy snow that clung to the posts, growing into horizontal
icicles on the lee side. there was always work to do and my
mother and i were always working. sometimes i'd look at
my little hands, wondering at those scabby things, too old
and worn for the rest of me. my face and hands may have
been rough, but the skin around my back and chest was as
soft and transparent as the inner bark of the mulberry, or

so my mother told me when she bathed me. once a month at night, as the wind moaned its way across the plains, ruffling the grasses with its million quick fingers, raising clouds of dust to the night sky, she would light a butter-lamp and pour a little hot water in a shallow tin tub. humming low tunes of sad-eyed men and their horses, she'd dab my naked body with warm water as i stood shivering in the tub, her cloth arcing slowly across my angular bones, tracing the fine-blue veins that snaked beneath my pale skin like river maps.

when my father came home from his long rides away, the wind was in the house for days, howling, yanking at our hair, sending things flying, putting dust in the air and scratches on the walls. then he'd leave and the wind would shriek out the door after him and be gone. as time passed he came home less often, then not at all. and from that time on it was only me and my mother and the wind in the grass.

today i walked with the sheep a long ways from the house, heading first up a slope on the hill behind the shed. there were no trees to be seen anywhere other than the wind-tilted persimmon that grew by the house, but across the plains there was nothing: no trees, no shrubs, just grass on rolling hills. so wide open. so empty. wherever you looked, you could look forever. from the top of the hill, the house with its sod roof looked like a mound of grass. if you didn't know, you might walk right past it. i led the sheep down the other side of the hill and began a long slow circle back to home that would take the rest of the day.

midday i sat to rest. the sheep lingered not far away, some laying down, others grazing. it was quiet and the sun was strong. i lay back in the grass and looked straight up at a sky so blue and so distant i felt like i would fall up into it. the grasses rose up around me, enclosing me, and i just lay there in a time beyond time, not a sound to be heard but the occasional bleat.

i thought about heaven. why it was blue.

i thought about the sheep. why they stayed with me instead of running away.

i thought about what might be beyond that point, way off in the distance, where the grass turns to haze.

it was so quiet and still, i could hear my heartbeat. and i thought about that.

so quiet.

then it struck me. i sat bolt upright. glanced around and cocked my head to listen. i listened so hard it was some time before i realized i wasn't even breathing.

the wind had stopped.

in all that vast rolling land not a blade of grass was moving. not one. as if all life and motion in the world had just blown itself out.

i stood and looked around. searching for any sign of movement. then i held absolutely still with my eyes closed to see if i could feel anything.

very quiet.
　　　　very still.

then i felt it once more. the wind. not outside, sliding across the land. it was right there, inside me. i could feel it, still blowing. *inside* me. not howling around, like wind in a cup. no, i could feel it moving in one direction through me. just like it did outside.

coming from nowhere.

going nowhere.

i was a childshaped piece of wind.

we know best what we are
when we are without

blue planet

dear cloud

i remember the first time i saw this planet, hanging off in the distance a cobaltblue ball frosted in violent swirls of pure white. how frightening. that color. that blue.
what could it possibly mean.

and those clouds.
you can't imagine how poisonous they look at first.

firefly

dear cloud

i have been a firefly. filled with the brimming winks of an incredible cool light. beating. beating. ever beating.

a hard, week-long rain had ended, stopping as suddenly as it had started. the white sound of water pelting on broad leaves lifting and fading into the jungle, replaced by a quiet just as deafening. the newly washed air was shot through with warm light from the setting sun, casting sideways through the trees. finding openings in the canopy here and there, beams of light probed deep into the tangled forest, illuminating the mist in long banded shafts, passing through the maze of trunks and hanging vines, cutting down into evermore complex lace-shadows the further in they reached.

i moved out of that dappled light and down to the banks of a dark river that flowed slowly through the endless trees, tracing lazy brown arcs, glistening, carrying hunks of the broken forest with it, whole trees drifting sideways, clung to tightly by small animals, their eyes wide and darting. high above, the remnants of rain clouds lay torn and scattered across the sky, edging in pastel hues that bled until the sky itself was stained in their soft colors.

those skycolors fell and caught on the skin of the river where they stretched out, rippling, wrapped like iridescent shawls around the leafy heads of the trees as they floated silently by, making their pilgrimage downstream. the rain gone, the quiet air began to fill incrementally with croaks and calls, busy chirps and clicks that carried back and forth, hesitant at first then incessant, rising and falling in waves. i breathed deep and slow, closing my eyes just to be able to open them again and discover, as if for the first time, this world of fluid color. it was a dusk to remember. a dusk to drink of, and stagger under its weight.

by the edge of the river a small motion caught my attention. a long blade of grass had curled over toward the river in a smooth arc and bobbed slowly as its tip touched the moving water, on again off again, nodding repeatedly. on the inside of that arced blade was a firefly, its light just barely glowing. an infinitely gentle light. i was drawn to it and merged, and as i did, the river and sky and all things big fell far beyond the horizon of my sight and all those jungle sounds bubbled up into a rumble like distant thunder, replaced by things more close and subtle — the scratching of small feet; the pasty chewing of small mandibles.

a long green snake slid through the thick riverbank grasses, passing just inches below me, its lithe tongue licking at the air.

the sun went down and darkness settled in, palpably, as if it were a thing being born from the very air itself, or stealing out of the jungle on padded feet. it purred down around us, filling up spaces that used to be, erasing them in a rising tide of emptiness. in the newborn darkness, i felt a twinge, an electric-tingle, and the hard sheaths over my wings began opening, slowly at first, just a crack, then closed, then opened, then closed again. they did this over and over for a few minutes and then with a sudden rush, they clicked upright and held there, poised. the delicate lace-like wings that lay beneath them, twittered and rose, timidly beating at the air. an urge arose in me. not a thought but a knowing. tense and full of purpose.

it was then that the many lights began, the cool beating lights. it came within me and, in others nearby that i hadn't noticed; a firefly just below me on the blade of grass, and two more just above. their silent lights began flicking on and off in staccato rhythms, irregular and pulsing, lighting the edges of the grasses like candles flickering in a cup. on again off again. coolly.

there is a moment when things begin. important things. tide changes. a moment that can't be foretold, only felt. and when that moment came, the four of us on that leaf by the river beat our wings in unison, released our holds, and fell slowly back into the air, humming up and down in lazy waves above the wet riverbank. our lights on again off again, coasting up and down, ever so slowly, lazy sparks in the night air, tracing along above the dark river. from right and left, from low and high, from every tree and patch of ferns nearby, other fireflies appeared, flowing down by the hundreds, then the thousands, then tens of thousands, all moving with the utmost disdain for purpose, bobbing this way and that, all careless and yet all tumbling along toward exactly the same place.

coasting above the muddy river, following behind the broken trees that rolled slowly in the wet darkness below, lit only by our flickering soft lights, fireflies flocked tipsy downriver toward a tree that hung out over the water and, once there, rose up and up for what seemed an eternity into that black web above us. up and up and into that huge tree we flowed like sparks up a chimney, catching up in the thick leaves, coating them with so many of us that bit by bit the branches sagged under our weight. the tree flickered with its new coat of lights. we were glitter, we were crystals, we were shoals of stars scattered in a tree-shaped galaxy, and we stared stunned at the blinking worlds that surrounded us. beating and beating, calling out into the night, *i am here, i am here, come, i am here,* over and over again without respite.

for hours we lay bunched against each other on every leaf and twig of that tree, blinking out our desire, and in imperceptibly slow stages we began to fall into the same rhythm, so that our lights no longer flickered but flashed, no longer sparkled but zapped, and the tiny little individual lightbeats that we had just been, coalesced into one solid silent thrum, flashing blindingly, over and over, minute by minute, hour after hour, drumming our lights into the night air, on again off again, burning straight down into the very core of our tiny awed brains the heartbeat of our universe.

i have never felt so completely part of the world

pond

dear cloud

i have been the mirror surface of a pond.

it was autumn when i first came here, when i first saw the pond nestled in the forest. the leaves of the birches on the other side were golden, their pure white trunks rising up through them by the hundred like so many strokes of chalk. from where i sat, on top of a large boulder — a colossal piece of glacial remain that rested on the shore like a beached whale — i looked at the forest not where it was but down below, in the water, upside down, reflected in the slowly rippling surface of the pond, the stands of white trunks and the hammeredgold patterns of autumn leaves spreading across the water like an oil slick. below them hung a clear sky banded by high cirrus clouds and line after line of black geese flying south. all this, upside down in the water, shivering when the wind gusted, the gold and white interspersed with charcoal shadows and undulating streams of electricblue.

all the world was there on that thin film that exists between water and air. all the world i thought, and i lay myself upon it, spreading out, stretching thinner and thinner until i covered every inch of that pond, the edges of me lapping lightly on every shore. at those far edges i trickled in between round pebbles of many sizes and colors, brown red and green, going in and out of them as i rocked.

i was in the pebbles. i was in the stands of cattails where black water snakes curled themselves before casting out across the open water. i was in the driftwood that piled up on the leeward shores, home to raccoon cubs that came to lick me with their gentle tongues. and across the breadth of me in between those shores, i held anything and everything that came before me, filling myself with them as easily as if colored by spilt ink.

i held the sun and the moon through their daily voyages.

i held the night sky filled past brimming with its countless stars and, once, a lone jet, high high up above blinking its way through the universe.

i held clouds and trees.

i held the hulking shape of a moose that waded into me to graze on water plants.

then the season turned, the nights got suddenly colder, and i froze, becoming a paperthin layer of crystal water still rolling on the movements of the pond below me. still giddy before the teasing wind, but now mute. the grey sky and leafless trees, the passing flocks of birds, all the things that used to glisten over me, now lay on me dully as a soft white light.

below, schools of small fish tapped away at me with their mouths as if looking for what had been lost.

this morning, a large goose came flapping over the bare birches and noisily circled the pond, dropping lower and lower as it flew through its incessant honking, banking once steeply on the wing and straightening itself for landing. the last few yards it held its wings out in stiff arcs and came gliding down, lifting its black webbed feet out in front of itself at the last moment. its back talons sliced through me and the weight of the bird opened a long gash in the thin ice as it sank into the cold black water.

the bird stayed quietly, sleeping for the rest of the day. the moon rose into an impossibly clear night, and when it finally flew away — startled by some noise and running on my brittle back, flapping with all its might to get airborne — when the goose flew, i flew with it, looking down as i circled higher and higher, the pond a dry circle of silver moonlight, with one long black scar like a smile. or a frown.

i was a mirror   and then i was not
     i was the place between two worlds
          and was nothing
               but what was laid across me

the touch

dear cloud

i have been a lonely man, a stranger all my life.

today was slow. all morning i sat on a rock on the edge
of a long straight road through the llano, a shadow under
the relentless sun, a dark spot burned onto the endless
brown grass, waiting for a passing car or truck to give me a
ride. few came. none stopped.

i've told you before of my life during the years i've
been who i am now, and nothing really has changed. i still
move around a lot, never stopping long in any one place.
never finding the things that would make a man settle —
money, friends, love. none of that.

i have, as they say, a bad face. i've told you that before
i'm sure. no? a bad face? i don't know. i don't look at it

myself anymore. but i think they're right. people shy when i talk to them. move away and whisper to friends, tossing their heads at me over their shoulders. i grew up too fast, outdoors a lot. i think i ended up on the feral side of possibilities. so i drift, nothing new, always halfway between running away and running to.

that's how it was this morning. sitting there on the rock, staring out across the barren landscape. i took a long slow breath. another second gone. the wind lifted and some loose brush skipped across the road. another minute gone. forever. just like that. like wind rolling across an empty land. the hours. the days. all the years of my life just flowing out and away. and gone.

it was hot already at dawn and grew worse through the morning as the sun rose high overhead. i pulled my hat down and dropped my face into its shadow. the sun rose and so rose a steady wind — not hard but constant — lifting a fine layer of dust a few inches from the ground and skittering it sideways across the land, hissing it through the patches of dry grass, over fields of pebbles, filling all the small hollows along the way. i looked down at my feet and saw small slopes of fine brown sand next to my shoes and realized i hadn't moved an inch in an hour.

i pushed my hat back up with a bent finger and looked around, squinting, breathing deep and slow against the heat. i would have spat if i had any. i brushed the fine grit off my shaggy moustache. it had the scent of dry grass, faintly, and something flatter like clay or ash. or the bitter smell of the sweat and blood of every man lost in this barren land who looked across it in despair. and now me. here. adding my own.

a gecko sputtered out from under a dry bush and drew curved strokes in the soft sand as it ran, disappearing into the shade of another, gone as quickly as it came, an apparition. leaving only those fine tracings as proof of its existence. the wind riffled across them and ten minutes later the lines were smoothed and gone. i've never left more behind myself. maybe less.

a buzzard traced lazy circles across the cloudless sky.

time passed like water drying off a hot plate. just like that. evaporating. gone.

looking down the road for any sign of a truck, the distance melted into wavering vertical sheaves of tan light, glossy and transparent. far off, deep inside that molten air, i saw a small shadow rise from the side of the road, wobbling and trembling as it stretched upwards from the ground like a flickering patch of dark smoke. the shadow rose and came forward, separating into two as it floated down the road toward me, emerging slowly from its own radiant chimera, bending and puckering, growing increasingly solid and taking on, at last, the shape of two children, a boy and a girl, walking single-file down the road.

they were a long way off. i squinted to make them out, to be sure they were real. satisfied they were, i took off my hat and beat the dust from my pant legs and shirt, slipped the hat back on and slid it back.

33

the children walked slowly, each carrying a bundle on their back that was as big as they were. they appeared young, just 8 or 9 perhaps, and were walking that dry road all alone, eyes down, dark hats pulled hard onto their heads against the sun and wind.

they approached without looking at me, without giving so much as a glance to acknowledge that they knew i was there. here we were, in the middle of the llano with no one else for miles in any direction, and they acted like i was just part of the rock i sat on. paid me no mind at all.

when they got close, i tapped the brim of my hat and said quietly, hello young ones. the boy stopped. if he was surprised that the rock moved, that the shadow by the road spoke, his face showed nothing. the girl who walked behind him, his sister i thought, continued up to his back and stopped as well.

they both wore roughly woven ponchos, thin and frayed at the edges, the once-bright patterns sun-bleached and coated with a layer of dust. their shoes were black, thick soled. old. the seam along the sole of one of the girl's shoes had popped and a toe showed through. she wore no socks. she kept looking at the ground and if she noticed me looking at her feet she showed nothing in her face but her toe pulled back into the shadow of the shoe like a gecko slipping under a bush.

their shoulders sloped under the weight of the packs making their bodies seem too small for their heads. impish. their faces were weatherworn. deeply so, the boy's face pitted with small purple marks and fine lines like some strange sundried fruit. the skin of his hands rough and hard, the fingertips and nails black from digging in the earth. the girl's face was ruddy, wind-burnt, her lips dry and cracked. both of them were expressionless. masks of themselves.

the little boy's head turned slowly toward me, face canted down, his eyes rolling up as if they were dark weighted marbles. he studied me but revealed nothing in his quiet stare. after a moment his gaze continued around to the girl who glanced up at him quickly then back at the ground, and then he turned back to me.

his face remained utterly distant, a blank slate upon which feeling had not yet been etched. we stood that way, all left unspoken, the wind perhaps speaking for us in hushed whispers, our eyes locked. was this hesitation from respect. a sense of deference to an elder. or was it, as they say, my bad face, staring down at him from the shadow of my broadrimmed hat. what did he see in this dusty man sitting on a big rock at the edge of the road somewhere in the middle of nowhere. he broke our mute trance, turned back to the girl and spoke a word in their tongue. she reached beneath her poncho and brought out a flask. the boy took it from her and stepped up to me, presenting it with both hands like a desert acolyte offering a chalice.

i accepted it, palmed off the metal cap, and took a quick draft. not water. it was astringent like crushed leaves. he took the flask back, had a sip himself and handed it back to the girl who sipped and tucked it away under her poncho.

i fumbled inside my sack, pulling out a wrapped bandana, and unfolded it to reveal a little stash — a few broken cigarettes, a small jackknife, and some hard candy wrapped in brightly colored foil. snatching two of the candies between my fingertips, i held them out for the children. the boy's hands slowly came together, clasping, knuckles interlocked and rising to his lips as if in prayer covering the whites of his teeth that had begun to show through a half-held smile, his upturned eyes widening. you would have thought i was offering them the keys to the city. or salvation itself. the candy wrappers glinted in the sunlight. he teetered there on the edge of the road like a man at a cliff. the girl, sensing something looked up too, and they both hovered there wide-eyed, motionless, two small hearts beating faster in the huge country with its wind and skittering dust and sun beating down like hot pellets. the boy glanced back at the girl for the briefest of moments and then took a short step forward to accept the candies. he handed one to the girl and they unwrapped them and slipped them into their mouths in one motion, each folding the bright wrappers neatly and tucking them away. the girl turned her face back down to the road. the boy sucked on his candy and as he did his eyelids closed and opened, slowly, like those of a person who sits after a long journey.

after a minute, the children jostled their packs back

and forth to get them set right again. the boy glanced back at the girl to make sure she was ready. she flicked her eyes at him then back to the ground. he looked up at me with his eyes only, his face kept shyly down, the whites of his teeth poking through a smile. he glanced back and forth between my eyes, studying them sharply like he might see something different between the two. quickly, sprightly, he stepped forward and took my right hand, the candy hand, in both of his. his hands so small so banged up — doll hands that had been used as a trowel. and yet, his touch so soft. his searching eyes round and glistening. it was a touch i had not expected and it took me by surprise, gentle beyond reckoning.

if he said thank you…. good day…. safe travels…. if he said anything on parting, i did not hear it. the wind and the land and the road, all these were gone, leaving nothing but his soft touch. he turned and left, walking up the road at the same slow pace with which he had come. the girl stepped forward to me, quickly, sprightly. her eyes remained fixed to the ground weighted by a thousand years of custom. she too took my hand in both of hers, lightly, so exquisitely lightly, like the touch of fine sand poured palm to palm. no more than that. her eyes flashed up to meet mine once, her lips pinched together, crinkled tight against a smile she willed not to be, and turned to follow the boy up the road, leaving a tingly sweet chill on the split skin of my hands, a feeling that swept up my arms and shivered down my back. i looked down to see where i had been touched, but found only my old hands.

i watched them walk away for the better part of an hour as they traveled that long road through the llano. slowly they merged back into one dark shape, began wavering and puckering in vertical sheaves of heat, rippling smoke-like, then sank down into the silvery sheen that coated the ground at the horizon like shadow melting into mercury and were gone. for a long time after that, i kept looking off in that direction. the sun lowered and cast its sideways light across a land turning warm twilight hues. it was a world lit from within, a place of wonder, under an endless bluebowl sky. fine shadows stretched off every rock and patch of grass, striping the ground, lengthening far into the east, and still i watched that empty road, the warm wind drying every tear before they could be.

i will leave the llano eventually i thought. however long it takes. i will make it through. and when i next stand among men, i will not be who i was. i have within me now a smile and a gentle touch and will keep them close as long as i live.

the world is a strangely balanced place
and pivots wildly on rare moments

hello?

dear cloud

silence

are you there?   cloud?

i can't help but wonder.

my thoughts flow within you, but you never answer. do you.

cloud?

silence

ok. i get it.

sea-cliff pine

dear cloud

i have been a windweathered pine clinging to a cliff by the sea.

the land there was gentle and rolling, grassy, broken by groves of scrub oak that floated in the windy meadows like wave-lapped islands. the meadows rolled ochre and sage for mile after mile toward the sea, and then without warning, disappeared, dropping cold-cocked off a sheer cliff that plummeted to the surf below. it was there that i made my home, between those rolling meadows and the endless ocean, at the top of that precipice, on the ragged edge of solidity and air, rooted in some deep-pitted outcroppings. where i grew, hanging precariously above the abyss, there was not a speck of dirt. just me, a gnarly twist of wood spiraling inexplicably out of solid rock.

my roots stretched deep into the outcropping, entering through cracks that ice and rain had opened, the tips of my finest roots no larger than hairs, squirreling themselves into impossibly narrow fissures, anchoring me to that wall of stone. the depths of the rock was always cool even in summer. and it always held a taste of water, some meager drops that bled down from above, even in the driest of seasons.

never much. never nothing.

where my roots twisted out of the rock into light they gathered in a knotted spiral, a rough-barked trunk off of which grew crooked, windblown branches tracing in ragged lines to leeward. in the warmest summersoft breezes, in the moody gusts of spring and autumn, in winter gales that wafted spitsalt up to coat me in white crystals, day and night all through the year, i lived with the wind. i was a blown thing, a frozen sketch of the flowing air. my trunk grew out of the rocks toward the ocean, leaping out to light and space. my branches grew back toward the land, like i had stepped out boldly into the air, then changed my mind. dramatic. comic. that was me.

mine was a frugal existence living off ocean mists and wind-blown dust. the occasional bird dropping. seeds hidden and forgotten by a mouse, left to rot and dissolve around my roots. did i mention that's how i got there. mouse litter. and the shape that i now hold, this stubby, tortured wreck of a tree, is not happenstance, but the direct result of the urges and appetites of the place i live in. as surely as waves deposit sand on the beach in layered rippled bands so too am i a deposition of this very spot. no seed of my mother dropped 10 miles inland would look anything like me. i am a careful record of the paucity of my life, and of every gentle tug or lash laid across me by the relentless wind.

just below my trunk was a cupped shelf on the precipice. a surefooted creature could make its way down around the outcroppings from the grassland to where my clustered roots grew, but no further. for all its severity, the spot i inhabited was in some ways a cozy pocket in a heady place. over the years, many have come and shared that place with me, for a minute or an hour, before heading back up to their lives on the flatland.

a snake slithered down and wrapped itself around my sloping trunk, scratching slowly across my rough bark to shed its skin, pulsing bit by bit forward out of its past, leaving a pale casting of what it used to be hanging from me to dangle and flutter in the wind. for weeks after the snake had gone, it was still with me. a hollow, parchment snake wrapped around my trunk. fluttering.

crickets joined me on autumn nights, chirping away at the ocean, as if it cared.

a lonely boy came in summers and rested himself in the crook of my roots, thrilling at the dizzy height of his perch, his tossled hair casting softly across my lowest branches. he would stroke me idly, snapping off flakes of rough bark, poking at drips of resin and sniffing deeply at his fingertips, the scent of the forest mixing with the ocean in his still gentle mind. he came to hide himself from the world beyond, staring out to sea for hours with a dreamy intensity. he came for many summers, his body growing heavier as the years passed, his skin rougher, his humming voice lower. and then his visits stopped. i guess he found what he was looking for.

an osprey used me as a perch from which to scout the coast, bringing back fish to shred on me between talon and beak. the last bits always stuck and dried in the sun. snake-skin. fishskin. even in my remoteness, i was a marquee of life's turns.

there has not been much for me here
    this life between stone and wind
        but in all these measures large and small

i am what has touched me

43

moon through clouds

dear cloud

i have been the jagged space between clouds through which the moon is seen.

an impossibly huge harvest moon slung low above the horizon, lusty red and rising, staining the clouds with coral rust.
an ice-cold moon, high on a winter's night, that silvers the frozen clouds.
a cat's claw moon on a night so dark, the clouds were just charcoal smudges rubbing out the stars.

i have been that hollow space
        and i have felt the wonder and dread
                of many sleepless eyes

bumble-baby

dear cloud

i have been a baby in love with an unformed world.

i was passing by a house in the country as a bumble bee bumbling its way from flower to flower. on the porch, placed nicely in a pool of warm spring sunlight that angled in under a shingle roof, was a wicker bassinet. hanging over the end of the bassinet were what appeared to be flowers spinning slowly in the breeze. a marigold. a sunflower. a rose. i bumbled over to them to find some pollen. inside the bassinet was a loosely folded pile of soft flannel cloth and peeking out through the cloth like a diver through its mask was the face of a plump baby. i left the bee and flowed in through the eyes of that smiling face.

in the baby, things felt right. so very justright.

i was warm. toasty warm. the sunlight gently heating my feet through the blanket.

i was full. a milkfed full. the butter-smell of a hard nipple lingering on my lips. lips that still made small sucking motions in the air.

and i was slightly drowsy, gurgling, sending little white milk bubbles up along my fat wet lips.

there was a sound of humming close by. a mother-humming, the kind that always comes around the time of suckling. there was a gentle creaking. how could i have guessed it was the wicker i lay in that made the sound as it rocked back and forth under my mother's hand. the creaking was a sound like so many others, that simply was. no reason or source. just there. and there was a buzzing. a very sharp buzzy buzzing that caught my drifting attention.

there was light streaming across the world and wonderful patterns of color floating around in circles. reds, oranges and yellows. turning lazily, a little out of focus. i reached my hand out from the blankets to touch the colors but they wouldn't be touched. apparitions. pigmented ghosts without meaning or location. simply somehow out there, drifting across the field of my vision. another enigma.

among the floating colors there was a fat black dot. somewhat fuzzy. somewhat buzzy. it moved around the floating colors and when it bumped into them, they jumped, and it buzzed even more. bump. zzzit. bump zzzit. i have to tell you i thought this was the funniest thing i'd ever seen. the spinning blossoms of color, rotating like soft-edged worlds around each other. the sunlight and shadow alternating, bright and dark, glinting and fading as the colors spun. and the black dot bumbling about in it all. i gurgled and chuckled and sent milky bubbles popping into the world by the dozen.

i could have stayed that gleeful baby forever, in rapture with an unfathomed world. what wonder in pure sense. such bliss before comprehension.

knowledge ruins everything

merging

dear cloud

this process of merging. this wonderful wonderful gift. the ability to slip into any form, occupy it from within, become what i come upon. what you have granted me is an endless source of wonder. i can't begin to express the joy that it gives me.

i see an eagle wheeling high above and i am it, the world turning small below me.

i come across a waterfall and i am that gushing cataract.

an elk, a worm, a piece of stone.

a dot of rain

my world is limitless because of you

and yet....   as easily as i slip in, i slip out.

nothing seems to hold me long.

perhaps one day i'll find something i stick to.

dear cloud

i have been moss in a mine, 500 yards underground, growing in the light of an old worklamp.

the lamp was a beat up thing, dusty and dented from years of hard use and rusty from more years of neglect since the mine was shut down. it burned round the clock, casting a bright pool of light on the wall just where it met the floor. the surface of the wall was gouged with hackmarks where men had dug through rock to make the shaft, leaving marks as frenzied and wild as bear claws on bark. the next lamps in the mine were a long ways down the shaft — one further up, two further down — nothing but distant glimmers from where i was and everything in between

49

was pitch black, as deep as the emptiness between stars.

where the light of the lamp fell most strongly on the wall, i grew thickly, fading to a mere skim of green at the edges where the light faded out.

no light. no me.

a few ferns grew up from my green padding, sprouted from spores that had ridden in on the torn clothes of blackened miners.

from invisible fissures, water trickled out of the rock face and glistened down the wall, wetting me before running into a narrow trough on the floor of the corridor and dribbling further down the mine.

except for the occasional fritz of the worklamp, it was absolutely silent. absolutely absolutely silent. nothing moved but the seeping water. even the air seemed frozen, moving neither up nor down the shaft.

somewhere, a thousand miles away, a nuclear power plant was humming, fissioning blurs of atoms to boil water to make steam to turn a generator to make electricity that hurtled down a wire to a transformer, then across a frigid wasteland to another transformer, to a hole in the ground where it came whipping down and down through angular mineshafts to the tungsten filament of this old beat-up lamp, which just hung there, tilted, blowing photons out onto the cave wall.

here in this strange silent underworld i, a gentle patch of moss, find myself the child of plutonium, a tiny cosmos existing exclusively beneath this 200 watt sun. i live at the mercy of the mine manager who, by what great plan i do not know, keeps the lights on even though this shaft is now unused. when finally he flips the switch, my world will fold back forever into night. but for now, i live, and bask in the bright silence of my personal sun.

      sprinkle light
          and life will follow

the dump

dear cloud

i have been a sprawling dump on the outskirts of a sleepless city.

a million sparks of life ebbed and flowed each day in that city, skittering about, shuffling here and there, some frenzied some slow, making things and gobbling them up at the same time. and each day, they took the hard bits that couldn't be digested and carried them out to me, casting them upon me as offerings.

the trucks arrived regularly with their burdens. the world was good. i swelled like any glutton.

at dawn, gulls and crows circled me in broken flocks of black and white, nicking the air with their constant bitching, and then descended for the feast, pecking and yanking at anything that looked like food.

rats that had spent the night scurrying about tasting morsels of this and that, madly frightened of their own footsteps, laid sleeping just below the surface in thousands of dens, safe in their architecture of empty boxes and slit cans.

later, the children came in their tattered clothes to find those things mistakenly sent to me as useless. plastic bottles. wire. the odd piece of clothing. they wore their work — a party mask, one brightpink sandal, a rainbow bracelet of telephone wire. the older carried the little ones on their sides, gleaning one-armed through my wonders.

in the middle there was the shell of an old car, tilted jauntily up toward the sky, half sunken in the mounting waste. it broke down in days long past and sat gutted, yesteryear's ship floating on yesterday's dross. the wires and tires, every bit of plastic and cloth, any working part, any broken part, had long since been stripped off. even the car's bright yellow paint was all but gone, glinting only in the crevices, the rest a pastiche of blistering rust.

at times small fires burnt in me, spontaneous from the heat of my compression or, more often, accidental from runaway campfires left unattended by the children at the end of the day. those fires gave off light and heat, the rich smell of melting plastic. the car too was burning, consumed by the unchecked ravages of oxygen, only more slowly. without the light. without the heat. it just sat there, passing in a cold slow burn from its mechanical shape into countless flakes of loose skin. the children boarded it and made revving noises in their skinny throats, driving through dreams of muscular power.

on some days i rested, smoldering, nothing to do but relax into my own methane spa.

on other days i took stock of myself, really looked inside and examined what made me who i was. and those were the days that stretched long in joy and misery. starting at the top where memory was fresh and apparent, and working my way down through all the years of stuff, to places where everything was softened with rot and only small fragments of what was, remained.

a small packet of handwritten letters, each beginning dearest mother and ending loving son, each carefully pressed, laid one upon the next and tied into a tight bundle with a gold and red ribbon, the last one on top embossed with its official military seal.

a napkin tipped with pink lipstick and red wine. a black streak of caviar.

a set of the encyclopedia britannica, just like at a bookstore, bound in leather straps and wrapped in black cloth, lined up in its entirety from a to z except for volume 25, shuválov to subliminal self. just the one i was needing.

a shoebox filled with crisp new bills, packed inside another box with underwear and socks, everything riddled with small holes. how did the children miss that one.

bags, wrappers, broken lamps, the tiny hand of a doll, its fingernail polish as yet unchipped, and infinite other bits of plastic.

to know, to really *know* the stuff that we are made of. isn't that why we look.

i was what was carried to me
less what was carried away

dawn

dear cloud

i have been a boy waking for the first time.

it was still dark and i still more than half asleep when i felt my father stir and rise to leave. my mother and sisters and some other young-ones like me lay curled in twos and threes wrapped in rough blankets on the packed-earth floor. i lay there and listened to him get up, taking in all the small sounds of the sleepers — low breathing like gently sighing breezes, the smack of a dry tongue, the soft brushing of a leg stretching. little sounds that were there and yet not. suspended in a slow awakening, i listened on the warm edge of sleep, where dreams are still alive and the world too tumbled and warped to be real. bubbles of unfinished thoughts rose up, transparent, empty of their memory, and floated off into the dark. through a cracked eye i could see the shape of the open door that looked onto the clearing in the forest. it appeared to me sideways as if *it* were laying down, lit barely by a feeble flickering from the cookfire outside. the firelight shimmied in through the opening, casting barely discernable waves across the woven branches in the roof and walls. the smell of burnt meat and smoke hung in the darkness, settling on things like dew. i licked my lips and tasted the fatty remains of the pig, closed my drowsy eyes and rolled my back against the warmth of my mother's breasts, her mouth close to my neck, breathing slowly. i could hear my own breath rustling in and out against the blanket. my eyes eased open again, just slightly, and caught the shape of my father weaving his way through the sleepers toward the door, the silhouette of his strong back and muscular arms, his long hair braided down one side of his head, a heavy stick in one hand. he paused at the opening.

i had heard him rise and leave each morning for the past few days, and wondered where he went, but each day i was drawn back under by warm currents and slept until the sun was well up. today, when he got to the doorway, i rose to follow, pulling myself up slowly through cobwebs of sleep, rubbing at my half-closed eyes, yawning, skinny legs wobbly. a thing half-formed like the soft body of a cicada as it emerges from its own shell as yet unhardened. i stood over my mother, hunched, balanced halfway between the warmth of the blanket and the cool morning air. my father's shadow slipped from the door into the darkness outside and i followed in halftrance, stumbling as quickly as i could so as not to lose him. i felt the tips of my mother's fingers stroke lightly at my ankle as i left and she called my name. not out loud but to herself. softly. just once. then i was gone.

i paused at the doorway, leaning my skinny shoulder on the tree-trunk that framed the opening. waiting. young-ones did not go out in the dark. we just didn't. i hesitated. the air outside was chilly, the first scent of autumn turning in the air, and i wrapped my arms around my naked chest, glanced back to where my mother slept but couldn't see anything in the darkness. a rising breeze nuzzled the leaves in the forest, covering all the tiny sounds of the sleepers with its rattle. it was like there was nothing inside at all. no sound. no movement. i looked back to see my father walking slowly across the clearing and found myself walking after him not quite forgetting that young-ones didn't go out in the dark.

the cookfire was in the middle of the clearing and as i passed it, i could feel the warm glow of the embers on my calves, touching me lightly. the dogs sleeping by the fire looked at me lazily, sniffed and laid their heads down again. i could sit here with the dogs. sleep again by the fire. that would be nice.

my father had already crossed the clearing to the edge of the forest and paused again without looking back. he was waiting at that dense wall of leaves, as if searching for a way in. i tucked my chin down, lips tightened, and strode quickly, reaching him just as he pushed into the thick brush which swallowed us both into its complete darkness. the leaves and twigs sprung and slapped against my face and arms, smarting. i felt suddenly awake. fear will do that to you.

once deeper in the forest, the brush thinned out and there was nothing but a cover of ferns on the ground beneath the thick-trunked old trees. it was too dark to see much but i could feel them scratching my calves as i walked. i followed behind my father by sound and by smell — his footsteps on the ferns, the sweat-smoke odor of his body lingering in the air in front of me. my feet slid across the ground, fingers darting around in front of me like antennae.

the land began to rise steeply and my breath became shorter and harder as we climbed the hillpath. above our heads, through the fabric of the forest leaves, a pale grey light could just barely be seen as the day eased to dawn. after a hard climb we wove our way through broken out-croppings of granite stepping out at the top into twilight on a wide open shelf of weathered stone. our lookout high above the valley. i sat next to my father on a fallen tree trunk and we watched as the day lightened. the textures of the forest in the valley far below us, and across all the hills and valleys beyond that too, began to take shape and color.

as the river that traced the valley below us caught the new light and turned pale-grey then silver then blue.

as flocks of crows rose from their nests by the hundred

and cawed down the valley in search of food.

as a light breeze began to push at the once still air bringing up the scent of the autumn forest and our distant camp fire.

as the sun crept over the distant mountaintop with a wink of bright light and slid it's way across the landscape to paint the world anew.

there, on that slab of bare stone thrust out above it all, the new light and the flocking birds, the scents and the small sounds, the slowly unfolding details of the valley, they all rose within me as they rose in the world. in all the days i had lived until then, had i never woken before.

there are moments when suddenly you are new
and it takes your breath away

things i like about this planet

lightning flashing between dark clouds, far away. silently.

*narrow canyons carved through solid rock, their empty shape
    as liquid as the water that ran through them.*

wasp nests.

the translucent green of young rice in summer paddies.

*waking on a morning when the first snow
        has whitened the peaks of the mountains.*

*mist hanging low over a lake,
    holding within it the sad cry of a loon*

dear cloud

i have been a cactus in the driest desert on earth.

animals in dry places often suffer. the bigger they are, the more so. when the sun bakes down on them relentlessly they burn and cower. when springs run dry, they parch then weaken, stagger til they stumble and die of exhaustion, alchemized in time into bleached bones by an unforgiving sun.

for me, the midday summer sun is nothing short of glorious, sweet honey for my feast. i drink of it until sundown and pray for more the next day.

when it rains, i flower, but until then i am my own spring and happy in my place. the sun rises at dawn already impossibly hot and continues to fire up through the day, at

noon becoming a clear white hole in an otherwise blue sky
that spits down a heat intense beyond imagining.
and i say *i like it.* hey, i like it a lot.
bring it on big guy. is that all you got.

call me sól

call me amaterasu

call me ra

the only thing i hate
is cloudy weather

things i don't like about this planet

haven't found anything yet

i'll keep looking though

scattering

dear cloud

i have been a mayfly, but not for long.

they only live for 30 minutes. i liked the idea of the brevity, that little delicate burst of existence. like ice crystals forming in a cloud and melting before they hit the ground, or plum flowers opening and scattering on a hot spring day. a lighting strike. now here. now not.

so, i merged with the mayfly as a naiad and, after the last molt, stepped out of my skin and stretched my wings, fluttering up over the water, humping helplessly in puffs of breeze that jittered across the pond. my wings were so delicate, so fine. ultra-thin membranes not so much solid as etched lightly onto the air. and i had two long, long tails, hair-like tassels that flowed behind me when i flew. a dandy i was and no doubt about it. and utterly complaisant. the wind pushed me up, and i went up, down and i went down, helpless to guide my own path. two puffs and i went up, up. three quick gusts and i went down, down, down, until i was fluttering just inches over the glassy surface of a pond. i could see myself, so pretty, so lithe, reflected in the water, fluttering along, higgledy-piggledy, lah-dee-dah, and then, vaguely, in the darkness of the water, back behind my own reflected loveliness, there appeared two beady eyes and two sets of little bony teeth, and the taut mirror surface of the pond stretched and shattered, giving way to a gaping wet mouth that shot up at me. i was lost in a darkness thicker than night and deeper yet.

there's a lot of that on this planet. it's all about eating and being eaten.

it's happened to me before, being eaten, but this time, instead of emerging and starting again, i stayed where i was. in the dark. in the fish. i remember after being eaten there was a closeness, and a wetness, and a downward squeezing. and then, after a time, a slow sense of dissolving, of losing myself bit by bit. losing myself as mayfly, gaining myself as fish. not disappearing so much as slowly, incrementally, changing bodies. like stripping and dressing at the same time.

in the moments after awakening as a fish, i remembered eating the mayfly. spurting up out of the water into the bright light, the gulp, the snap, and a taste part tissuey (that would be the wings) and greasy (the intestines i guess) and very, very sweet. or not *sweet* but like sweet. anything that animals need most tastes sweet to them. that's what *sweet* is. the taste of what you need.

my life as a fish was fun. all silver flashes and bursts through quick currents, darting under rocks and through forests of waterweeds. biding time in still eddies, then fast across a stony brook, out into the air to gulp more bugs, quick along the bottom for nymphs. in a couple of days, most of the mayfly that i had been was absorbed into the new me, although some passed out in a long green-brown thread that trailed behind me attached for a while and then broke off, settling among the old rotten leaves that gathered in the gravelly mud at the bottom. there was a sense of thinning. i was there, now as fish, but not *all* there. not anymore.

as i said, my life as a fish was fun, but so was it brief. one day, as i was darting around, nabbing nymphs and bugs, i leapt and gulped and the air gulped back. i found myself sailing upward in the beak of a tern. the world below was bright and clear, so new seen looking upside-down from high above, a beautiful, blurry landscape, that swirled around and around, further and further below. the tern bit harder, i snapped, and then i was no more. in time, it landed, put me on a rock and ate me piece by piece.

over the next few days, again in measured stages, i

reawoke with beautiful wings and fine feathers of white and black, and a sharp red beak. terns are wonderful things. boy can we fly. our wings are like supple fans but strong — and we can flap like there's no tomorrow. pole to pole, north to south and back, non-stop flying.

i awoke as a tern, but not all of me was there. some had been left on the rock for a brown ferret to nuzzle and lick in the mist at dusk. some fell as white-brown streaks as we flew north over dark fir forests, falling and breaking into little droplets that scattered across a wide patch of moss at the edge of a clearing, near clumps of saxifrage and poppies and dwarf arctic azaleas. the saxifrage was a shameless flush of lavender blooms. some of me fell into the open flowers, some fell on the moss. i flew north, a paler me, watered down by all my changes.

near the artic circle, i flew into an ice storm, and was pelted by hard driving hail. the sharp balls hit like hammers out of nowhere and my neck broke with a little electric crunching sound. i spiraled down in long dizzying sweeps five hundred feet to the ground hitting with a whoosh and a plop. the next day, a brilliant clear morning, my body was found by a pack of white fox cubs with downy fur and round black dots for noses. they fought over me and i ended up in little pieces, some eaten, some strewn thanklessly across a hundred square yards of snowy tundra to be chewed into smaller and smaller pieces by smaller and smaller things until there was no more.

dear cloud, i felt so dilute, so ghostly, so little like

myself. and, this is the strange part, at the same time, i felt so big, so broad, touching so many things at once. there i was, on a cool streambed becoming a hundred nymphs nibble by nibble, in an tense ferret that pranced through the underbrush like a looping shadow, in yards of moss spiked with pearls of dew, bathed in the purple light that bounces around the inside of a saxifrage flower, and in six frisky pups with their sharp little fox teeth and pink fox tongues.

i'm sure if i kept this up i would disperse further and further afield, a little bit here a little bit there, until i was both nothing and everything.

it took me a month to pull myself together

dear cloud

i have been a quiet village, sleeping, at the bottom of a lake.

i have been the stone and clay houses with their peaked thatched roofs and small windows, empty wood frames like blank eyes. i have been the old stone walls that circle the courtyards, patched grey and white with lichen. i have been the footpaths and the rickety fences that line them, the old tools and broken furniture that lay about, idle. i have been all that and more, all the parts large and small that made the village what it was. but i have not been the people of the village. for they were gone by the time i came.

i was there when the waters began to rise, lapping up the valley from the dam, the river that traced the bottomland running hastily into a mobile delta that edged forward to consume what fed it. all of the bits and pieces of life in the village slowly disappeared beneath the flood waters, succumbing in order of their height. first the dirt paths that meandered through fields and the close-packed homes, edged with tufts of wildflowers and grass, patches of thistle with their prickly leaves and flowerheads. paths that were not so much built as spontaneous, unwitting records of the many daily comings and goings through the village, earthbound scrolls written with the soft pads of sandaled feet.

after the paths, the grey stone walls disappeared, the gaps between the stones filling like so many small harbors, the flood tides within them lapping and sucking at their shores. the makeshift pole-gates in the walls that closed the courtyards to people in the day and wild boar at night swayed gently in the rising water making soft thunking noises as if tapping out time. then the walls of the homes themselves sank below the surface, the water lifting higher inch by inch up along them to the eaves until all the low things of the village were gone, hidden beneath the water, and the village became an archipelago of thatched roofs clustered in the middle of a new-born sea, the steep upward domes of thatch reflecting downward in the still water. roofs floating in a glistening pool of sky and summer clouds, moored boats awaiting the signal to depart on a long journey. then finally the roofs too sank below the rising waters leaving only the tops of the tallest trees that had stood near the village, looking lost and confused, until they too succumbed and all that remained was a quiet lake framed by steep-sloped hillsides, pristine yet unnatural for its lack of beaches.

beneath the water, the village lay silent, appearing even as it had the month before, only empty. the paths and stone walls, the homes that lined the lanes and alleyways, the pole fences and racks for rice-drying all still there, suspended in their new, aqueous atmosphere.

streams of bubbles rose to the surface from all the buildings and stone walls, from upturned carts and piles of old possessions left behind. from the lips of one old man who had made a small pretense of leaving, then returned to lay in his bed and await a new life in his old home. bubbles from all over the village rose in torrents at first, then slowed to thin trails and finally ceased altogether except for the occasional times in the months following, after the earth had soaked and softened, when a tiny trail of bubbles rising from the ground would mark a spot where on a some distant moonless night now long forgotten a secret cache had been hidden in a hurriedly dug hole. a box of jewelry. a stack of banned books. a just-born girlchild, washed and wrapped in white muslin, still curled in fetal sleep.

beneath the water on cloudy days, everything was green-tinged and flat, a wet painting of a village more than a village itself, but when the sun was shining above the lake, beams of bright light would probe down through the water, casting shadows off the buildings and drowned trees. on those days the village seemed still as it had been, simply waiting, as if holding its breath.

the better homes had been made of stone and brick, the poorer ones of soil. those simple homes sat as they were for many months, the wattle and daub that made up their walls absorbing their fill of water, gluttons to the point of bursting. then one by one, when some unwritten law of tipping points had been breached, the softened walls would no longer support their roofs and collapse into themselves in slowly unfurling clouds of brown silt that would rise, mushroom and settle, leaving only shapeless heaps.

there was a chair in one home that floated to the ceiling as the green waters rose, and held there by its own buoyancy for weeks. then, waterlogged and weighted, it slowly sank, drifting down through the room, bit by bit as if lowered on fine strings, past the carved railing of the stairs, past a family portrait on the wall now softened and blurred like an old memory, past the sturdy plank table where so many generations had shared their meals and conversations, its edges rounded from the touch of many hands, settling finally on the floor by a small window that looked out across the valley. sunlight would stream in the window on clear days, lighting the fine silt in the water, warming the chair-seat and the floor, just like in the old days. a comfortable spot waiting to be enjoyed.

outside the window there was a well, its deep

stone-lined shaft, once so precious to the village, now but a weak spring of fresh water beneath the deluge, some small tears welling up into an ocean.

beyond the wellhead lay an orchard, its plum trees barren of leaves, shed for the last time by that endless liquid autumn, the leaves dropping even before they colored. amid the twisted black plum branches, schools of small brown fish swam where flocks of sparrows had once flown, drifting and darting, nuzzling through the tufts of green algae that clung to the branches like the upturned panicles of dark flowers. and beyond the orchard, at the bottom of the valley, the riverbed remained, its banks and boulders still visible, the old stone bridge still vaulted across the center stream, large stepping stones leading up to it on both sides, a group of willows hanging from the bank, leafless in the green-hued winter. at once empty and filled, the river was a perfect casting of itself, all the eddies and pools, cross-currents and down-drifts still apparent in the patterning of the stones that lay exposed. a dry riverbed running at the bottom of a lake.

over time i imagine, silt will settle bit by bit and the edges and outlines of the village will soften and sink into obscurity. but for now it remains, a place cast in murky crystal, lived in by new settlers with no sense of where they are.

falling through bed

dear cloud

i have been a woman with a hole in her bed.

this woman was well-known in her city; a person of
great wealth and fame. she spent her days, or what was left
of them by the time she rose, prowling the grounds of
her hilltop villa, appearing each night on the veranda to
gaze down on the glimmering lights of the restaurants and
shops on the quay, and the inky bay sparkling with schools
of anchored yachts. i saw her first from the narrow back-
streets, when i looked up by chance at that villa perched
high on a bluff above the slums, and caught a wraithlike
motion in the darkness appearing just briefly in the light

of the plateglass windows. from that night on i watched. each night she would appear, and each night i would move closer. as i neared, she alchemized incrementally into real form, shadow solidifying into woman. straightboard back, insolent thighs pushing at a skin-tight dress, a willow hand cradling a tall mojito, straight blonde hair falling like a guillotine down one side of her face, a thin red scar circling her wrist like a bracelet, greygreen river pebbles for eyes. when i got close enough to see the downy white hairs on the nape of her neck, i merged.

my days were filled with nothing, empty as the unused wings of my rambling home. when sweet ennui soured to tedium, i threw extravagant parties, stalking through crowds of well-oiled admirers leaving ruby kisses on more cheeks and crystal than i could count. when people started to bore me, i would lock the doors, curl into an armchair by the great fireplace in my library, watch flames crackle around oak logs and stroke my blue abyssian until its fur grew thin. party or no party, in the deep hours of the night, alone, i would make my way to bed. always alone.

last night, when the evening had played out and the pitchblack had just begun to give way to the herald gray of morning, i went to my bedroom, undressed and slipped naked between the fine silk sheets. laying perfectly still, i looked up at the ceiling listening to the tender noises that appear only at those times — a barely audible creak of the floor boards, the hiss of a steam radiator like an old man whispering in the next room, a fog horn wafting up from the bay as drawn out and forlorn as the howl of a lost coyote. arranging myself in bed like the dead, on my back, hands crossed one over the other on my chest, head poised, legs long and straight, i lay and waited. slowly the bed warmed to my body, the small sounds lengthened and stretched along a thin horizon, and the soft lights that glimmered across the ceiling paled. everything seemed to grow slow and soft around the edges and, as on every night before, i felt the hole in the bed ease open and my body slip slowly back into it, sinking like a bag of stones into quicksand.

i fell backwards, floating down through the bed ever so slowly, easing down through the floor of my room, then rolling and looping as i fell down through many other floors in succession like descending in an open-cage elevator through the alternating light and dark of an old apartment building, passing through the rooms of dreamers and lovers and crying babies, lower and lower, down through the checkerboard marble lobby to the basement with its cobwebs and wheezing steam boilers and lower still to a huge underground room filled with water, dark and still. into that water i went, sinking deep below the surface.

the water was black. what could be seen — the vague edges of distant shapes — was silver and platinum, moonlight colors. i floated down through that limitless dark pool, huge charcoal flowers rising up around me, black on black, edged in thin lines of pale light. i swam through forests of flowers taller than me, body arching in otter-waves, bubbles trailing out of my mouth and hair, leaving iridescent pearlclouds in my wake. the flowers began opening and closing like the mouths of sea anemones, puffing at the water. inside them were stamens covered in bright red pollen, luminescent in the darkness. the flowers were puffing and puffing, drawing me closer, sucked in by the rhythmic motion, the stamens wiggling and stretching lewdly in and out of the black flowers, red edged in silver, wiggling and stretching. wiggling and stretching.

i was standing at the edge of a sand beach, the water lapping at my ankles. stretching out behind me was the ocean going on forever. in front of me, on the other side of the white sand, fine as baby powder, was a jungle, a solid wall of layered botanics. a river came rushing from under the leaves, pouring fully conceived out of nowhere, a fountain from the forest. next to the river, all but hidden in the large overlapping leaves, was a little girl, her face a white dot in the green brocade, her eyes dark circles. she was looking directly at me and all i could see was those eyes. sad, sad little oceans held tightly within the deep hollows of her face.

the girl and i were walking up the stream through the jungle. she was very strong. man strong. her hand like a vise on mine pulling me forward incessantly. the stream was rocky but her feet were sure. she moved with ease, i stumbled. branches and vines hung across our way but she moved lithely under them and around them, cat-like, never pausing. i tangled and faltered, her strong hand yanking at my wrist each time i did. light came down to us sporadically in quick shafts through the thick overhead canopy. the air echoed with animal grunts. monkeys. i looked up but saw instead well-dressed men, rigged in tuxes and cummerbunds, hair slicked back with tonic, hanging from high branches, flailing their arms, pounding their chests and hopping up and down like satanic revelers, screeching, scratching their butts and well-shaven faces and flashing their eyelids and teeth while their heads snapped around on their necks. they tore branches off the trees and threw them down at us, whole arcs of leaves rattling and shivering from their frenzies.

i was in a long hallway of an old academy, dark wood wainscoting and gaslights on the walls. i thought i knew the place. my old school? light came in from high windows that lined the hall, casting pale rectangles diagonally across the stone floor. my shoes made clicking sounds as i walked down the hall, precisely and evenly, like a metronome. behind each door i passed, people were whispering. i could hear them but i couldn't tell what they were saying. at the end of the hall one door was open. i went in. there was an old four-post bed in the middle of the room. nothing else. gauze netting covered the bed like a tent. someone was sleeping inside, their heavy breath audible as i approached.

i pulled back the netting quietly. clear light seemed to spill from the opening, as if the gauze were releasing what it had been holding back. beneath the thick white comforters, nestled in overstuffed downy pillows, was the face of my mother, silver-haired and pale, as wrinkled as an old fruit. i spoke to her. if she heard, she didn't answer. i slipped in next to her under the covers, her incensed smell on me like a gloved hand. i lay still for a moment next to her, then the bed opened and i fell through.

the clearing in the jungle was devoid of any plants — nothing but packed red clay on the ground. it was night. in the center of the clearing was a crowd, all gathered around a fire, staring down at it. the little girl was there, too. i pushed my way through the gathered people. no one seemed to notice me. in the middle, near the fire, the faces were lit up with flashes of red and yellow light rippling up over them in waves. their heads moved in quick excited jerks. in the fire were pieces of meat, sizzling and hissing with little pops and snaps. with each fizz, the crowd gasped and pushed in. there were ribs and claws and a hoofed leg sticking up, and packs of little hands wrapped in leaves. little baby hands. i was hungry. i'd never been so hungry.

we were all eating, ripping the hot bloody flesh from the bones with our teeth. everywhere was the sound of smacking tongues. i felt someone looking at me from across the crowd, turned and saw my mother's face, deathly pale, just staring and staring. she seemed so disappointed with me. so disappointed. i hung in mid-bite, hands dripping with grease, a tendon pulling away from my teeth. i looked down at the meat and back but she was gone.

i was running through the jungle. breathless. my mother appeared in quick glimpses through the trees ahead. the little girl was pulling her by the hand. they ran so quickly. so easily. as hard as i ran i couldn't seem to catch up. i couldn't get closer. well-dressed men high in the trees were screeching and yapping, their fevered voices rising in crescendos. one of them had a girl in a silk dress bent over a branch, a long string of pearls hanging from her neck. he had her dress pulled up, her naked ass bright red in the sunlight and was humping her as hard as he could from the back. the other men in their fine suits and white starched collars clung to trees around them pointing, screeching and yapping, their perfect white teeth chattering, flapping their arms around like rubber sticks, hopping up and down, shaking showers of twigs from the trees.

i was in an open meadow on top of a hill of grass. the land fell away in all directions. it was like standing on top of a huge overturned bowl. my mother and the girl were far down the hill, appearing and disappearing behind boulders. i ran, trying to call out but my voice caught in my throat. the hill got steeper and steeper, the land falling away like the listing deck of a capsizing ship until i was pulled forward by my own weight unable to stop. i ran as fast as i could just to keep from falling and called to my mother, screaming, but there was no sound and she was so far away. the meadow kept tilting, so steep it was almost vertical, a cliff of green grass. my foot caught on something and i went flying headfirst tumbling and tumbling, hacking at the grass with clawed fingers trying franticly to find something to grab on to but i just kept skidding, rolling out of control, falling, turning and turning and turning, coming up at last wet with sweat, tangled in sheets and clinging to my own torn pillow.

an old man whispered something in the next room.

i lay for a moment rigid, wide-eyed. then let go a long sigh. my muscles relaxed and i sank back into the pillow, breathing deeply of the coffee and bacon frying for breakfast downstairs. the radiator in the next room hissed.

aren't dreams wonderful

reception

dear cloud

   i send my thoughts to you

      you never answer

         why

   is it poor reception

      perhaps i should try the other side of the planet

curling

dear cloud

i have been a fern unfolding.

in a forest of deep slanting shadows, close to the ground with its many tiny scratchings and slitherings, surrounded by the steady rumble and rush of a waterfall, i was a fern. in the early spring, as the frozen ground melted and water wicked up through the deep soil, with the sputtering sucking sounds that springwater makes, as the sun streamed through jagged webs of naked branches casting thousands of black lines across the mossy ground, as hundreds of tiny creatures scurried about with their busy preparations, calling awake!, awake! with their many little noises, i lifted my furled head from the forest floor, rising slowly, a coil of life unwinding toward light.

the motion was so graceful. this rising and outward

rolling, expanding and opening, beginning as a clasped inward thing and ending fine and frail and stretched out to the sky like an opened palm.

summer came and i hardened and thickened, autumn tinged the edges of my leaves with bronze and russet, and as winter set its frigid nights upon us, i withered, my stalk weakening until i bent, curling up on the ground, brown and dry.

i have been a fern.

i have been a kangaroo pup, just born and twined around a teat in my mother's pouch.

i have been a spider, dried by desert winds, tucked behind a rock on a high stony plain, pulling slowly into myself, balling up to die and be blown like tumbleweed from stony pocket to stony pocket.

i have been an infant snake, wrapped around itself twenty times inside an egg, unreeling through a hole in the soft shell.

i have been a jacamar chick that fell from its nest and broke on the ground, my wings folding ever tightly around myself with my final breaths.

i have been many things. around here, you begin curled. uncurl. and curl again at the end.

> it is the way of things
> in and out
> like breathing

dear cloud

i have been the place where water falls from.
  not the water but the place.

  a river had cut its way down through the millennia, carving through layers of hard and soft rock that had been set down in ages past as mud on an ocean floor, until it flowed through a narrow gorge of its own making. reaching a fifty-foot cliff where the land had been dug out deeply by a glacier, the rushing water leapt straight out for a yard or two as if it hadn't noticed and then fell straight down in long white strands that frayed into clouds of floating spray.
  i was that place. the cliff and the high walls of striated rock that framed the spouting water. the opening. the orifice. a gate teller on a highway watching life go by.
  in autumn, fallen leaves would coat the water, brocades

of red and golden warping as they flowed downstream over hidden stones, then casting out into the air in front of me, confetti in celebration of the season.

spring floods would bring broken sticks and mounds of grasses, dry refuse of the winter past, branches, broken trees knocking and battering their way to me, leaping out over the precipice, forests tumbling from the sky.

mudslides upstream would turn the water blood brown. in the heat of summer it was algae green. on clear days blue, when overcast the grey of arctic seas. under a full moon, quicksilver. a rainbow river no two days the same. in winter the top froze solid. what water came, came from below, sliding out from under the thick lid of ice and over the edge, cascading along the long white beard that grew down from me.

in the hundred yards before it reached me, the river ran deep and smooth, its surface a mirror, reflecting everything within sight — the scaled stone walls along its banks, the sky overhead with its ever-changing clouds, the twisted black branches of overhanging trees. but just where the water passed me, where the river reached the edge of its solid bed and cast recklessly into emptiness, at that point between languor and tumult, the smooth river bent, curving downward as it fell, and all the world it held — the sky and the clouds and the branches with their perched songbirds — warped and stretched into wild elongations of themselves, everything going mad, expanding, breaking up, and finally exploding into droplets and disappearing.

and, as i watched those beautiful reflections throughout the years, squeezing the flow between my stone hands and letting it cascade away so elegantly, as i watched, so too did i join, dissolving into the water, chipping away grain by grain, and passing downstream with the rest.

> i shaped a world
>> that was shaping me

the path

dear cloud

i have been an old woman, living on my own.

i was from a small village high up in the mountains, secluded, surrounded by jagged peaks which stayed white through the year. should i say village or hamlet. i'm not sure what to call it but it was nothing to speak of. a few families, our small homes, some chickens and the fields.

there was but one path that went down the valley to what lay beyond. whatever that was, i didn't know. i had never been there myself, but anyone who left, left that way and anyone who came, came in from there.

i worked a small plot of land on the edge of the village, growing vegetables and some barley that the boys would harvest in the autumn. the path down the valley ran along my field, and from there twisted its way between strewn boulders, across a rickety wooden bridge over the quick falling stream, and then disappeared into a dense stand of deodars. as i grew older, my life came down to three things — my home, my field, and the path down the valley.

when i was a young woman, things were very hard in our village. the crops had failed twice and my husband went off with a few other men to look for work. he had heard from those who came back from the market town that two week's walk from where we lived, a canal was being built. a huge project. any man who was fit to work could find it. my husband and his brother and two others from the village talked late into the night, night after night, and in the end decided to go. they left early on a clear morning, full of bright hopes and good cheer. we waved colored cloths and sang as they left. i followed them as far as our field, waving and singing and then stood there continuing to wave, continuing to sing, watching them walk down the path to the forest. i can still see my husband strolling down that path, one arm thrust out of his sturdy robe, his white sleeve bright, catching the sunlight one last time before he slipped into the shadows of the trees.

in the years that followed, i would look up from my work in the field — hoeing the furrows, weeding, gleaning grains — and stare down that rocky path to where it bent around the corner and disappeared into the deodar forest, into the endless darkness of that place. i would pause my work and peer deep into that darkness for any sign of movement no matter how small. a glint of light, a rustle of leaves.

many years later, one of the men who had left, one of the friends, came back to the village. he was very tired-looking. very thin. he spoke but little and nothing of consequence. please forgive me. please forgive me. this he said over and over in a low voice, slowly, as if weighted beyond bearing. he never said why.

i raised our three children as best i could. some of the others in the village would lend help, but there was little to go around in the best of times. four or five years after my husband left, one of our young men came back from the town carrying a long gun. everyone was so excited. we had nothing like that in the village. it was new and so fine. the boys would watch him shoot targets in the fields, their faces blank with awe, flinching at the sound then quickly recovering and posing bravely. he told many stories late into the night with the boys of the village gathered around him in the firelight. great changes were afoot in the world, he said, the moment was upon us. the brave would fight and prove themselves heroes. when he left some days later, my eldest son left with him. it was late spring. the wildflowers were running mad in the meadows. they were so beautiful. i looked across them slowly. high up on the slope, a rangy grey wolf loped along the edge of the forest. he turned and sniffed at the air, and looked down at me from high above. i thought he was looking at me. i don't know. i just remember those crystal wolf eyes, staring down from so far off. as the boys began their journey, we all gathered and sang songs, waved brightly colored cloth. i too sang but not so loud this time. the boys swaggered down the valley and i watched them cross the bridge, turn the corner, and sink into the depths of the deodars like stones into a pond.

the seasons passed. summer came all too briefly. the hills turned a brocade of gold and soon fell to sleep beneath their winter covers. spring came, and then another and another and another. what little news we heard of the fighting was not good. never good. and then no more. it had all ended. all those years, i imagined my son proud and tall upon a horse surrounded by other strong men. i imagined him dead, cold, grey and bloodied on some distant barren field, his mouth open and filled with dirt. i would sit on the banks of my field and look as far down the path as i could see, peering into the forest like a hunter, and imagine everything good and everything bad and everything in between.

in the year of the ox, as winter settled in with its first blizzard, the landscape paling to white on white, the whole world lost in a dizzy sideways flow of snowflakes, an old lama struggled up the path to our village seeking shelter. my husband and son being gone, it was decided he should stay in my home, which was a blessing on us and gladly received. it was a hard winter, the hill-passes too deep with snow to cross, and in the end he stayed until spring. he was a stern man, grizzled, white hair cropped close, with large drooping ears. he had with him some scrolls of the scriptures and the village would gather with him for a few hours each day to hear him recite and expound. winters here usually pass so slowly with so little to do. his being with us was a joy and we all felt richer for it. he shared his thoughts with all who came, freely and equally, but since he stayed in our house, he took a little extra time to guide my younger son with his studies — reading, writing, and understanding the way. in the evenings, i would fix them bowls of buttered tea, and by the soft light of the lamp my son would unfurl the scroll to where he had left off last, and begin to chant. the lama sat nearby, back against the wall, eyes closed. if the boy hesitated or erred, the lama would chant a few lines to set him back on track. my daughter and i sat across the small room, mending things or weaving her marriage apron for the eventual day. in the spring, as heavy snow melt filled the stream to overflowing, sending it in cascades down the valley, the lama left with my son on his heels, his head newly shaven. they chanted as they walked. i followed a ways behind them to our field to watch them go. new shoots could be seen popping in the meadows. the swollen buds of the birches cast a red haze over the hillsides. i did not sing. i did not wave any bright cloth. my daughter close at my side, i watched them trundle down the rocky path, their voices, one low one high, floating back up intermittingly on the spring breeze. they crossed the old bridge, turned the corner, and slipped into the shadow of the trees. for just a minute after that, i could still hear their voices. at least i thought i could. it may have been the wind in the trees. then they were gone.

since then, i have watched the path and waited. i might be planting seeds, nightingales flying down from the hillsides to scold us in the fields, and i would see something out of the corner of my eye and glance up, and find myself still looking down the path a long time later. or it could be during a midday break. i'd be leaning back against a bank to rest in the warm summer sunshine. i would sip a little tea from a gourd flask, and my head would roll to one side just to see. looking way way down that path. just to see. as the birches that swept up the hillsides slipped into their gold vestments, i would follow the orbits of a griffon high above, watch it circle its way over the village and down the valley, and end up staring down the path, hardly breathing, just staring a hole in the trees. even in winter, when i had no earthly business going to my field, i would wrap my legs in straw mats and wade out through the drifts, pretending to myself i was planning next spring's crop and find myself leaning on a stick, looking for a long, long time down the trackless path, snow gathering lightly on my shoulders.

today i rose at dawn as i always do, made a flask of
tea, and walked to the field. there were so many weeds to
pull. where do they all come from. i pulled them all. it was
a good day's work. i am old, but i can still work a full day
and that feels good. as i stood to make my way home, pick-
ing up my old hoe and rusty sickle, i looked down the path
once more and saw nothing but trees.

i thought to myself.... i thought, it must be tomorrow.

and nodded to no one, yes, tomorrow.

i have come to know
the elasticity of hope

nebula

dear cloud

i think of you often.

i imagine you as a nebula, an immense celestial cloud, dark and brooding yet filled with an inner light, growing larger and larger as you gather more and more information from all the long distance travelers like me, swelling with the knowledge of the cosmos.
i have heard when a nebula grows large enough, it eventually collapses into an infinitely dense singularity, and a new star is born.
and you? when you have filled to bursting with all our many memories and expanded past a certain tipping point, unknown perhaps to even you, will you too fall in upon yourself.

and what then.

first blood

dear cloud

i have been a hungry cheetah.

when i merged, i found it had been long since i last ate. i was lolling in the crotch of an old tree, high off the ground, the maze of fine black branches like twisted wire above me providing only a suggestion of shade, drawing a net of lines across my spots. my body lay slung across two branches, head resting heavily on one, legs dropped, limp, four dead weights, tail twitching high in the back like some separate live thing. sleep had been good at first disturbed only by the occasional whiff of lion on the night air, but napping was losing its appeal and the scent that had my tail twitching now was not predator but prey.

it was morning and i was hungry.

what was that smell. dik dik. kudu. gazelle. yes, gazelle.

i could smell their sweat and dung in brief drifts on the faltering wind, faint and far away, blended with the dust of the savannah and the warm grasses, but as the morning passed and the herd moved closer their odors became undeniable. my eyes clicked open and my head rotated to windward. no other part of me moved. my legs remained hung, body limp. only my head was erect, suddenly intent.

there. far away. those black stripes like fallen branches in the grass. there.

i slipped from the tree to the ground and loped toward the gazelles. slow and low, body stretched out straight. the closer i got, the lower and slower i walked, dropping and freezing each time the gazelles so much as flinched, finally nestling into a stand of grasses and lying down to wait.

when the gazelles had grazed their way to within striking distance of where i lay hidden, i sprang, aiming for one young buck. startled, the buck turned on its hard black hooves and bolted, right, then left, then right, digging into the soft soil and banking wildly to avoid me. as i ran behind it there was nothing in the world for me but the white flash of its haunches and flapping black tail, the panicked jittery running, the smell of piss and sweat. my lungs filled, pressed, panting as i ran, heart beating heavy in my ears, claws tearing at the earth. and when i was close enough to hear its short gasping breath, i lunged and sunk my sharp dew claws into it flanks, yanking it to the ground, then threw myself on top and bit down on its throat. it kicked me several times as hard as it could, then a few more times weaker, then not at all, one wide glazed eye looking straight into mine, a polished black horn glinting, blood gushing warm into my mouth.

i waited until the gazelle was completely still, and then tore into its flesh. sweet red meat still flinching at my bite.

there was not much time. i could see hyenas far off on a rise and it would not take them long to get here. when they did, i'd need to leave. but for now, eat. eat and enjoy.

today i learned the pleasure of killing

and a great pleasure it was indeed

inner light

dear cloud

i have been a mute cylinder of aluminum filled with jellied gas, loosed onto a jungle village.

i was quiet. i was a tuned chord yet to be struck, hanging entirely inert, bolted to the underside of the wing of an f100, a silvery squeeze of metal tapered on both ends, elegant and honed, slipping through the cold air at 5,000 feet like a blown whistle. the plane banked and fell, nose-diving at the earth, screaming, tracing a long bell-curve through the air, and dropped me at 200 feet before returning to thinner altitudes.

i fell, tumbling wobbly and unsure, tracing an irregular downward arc that mirrored the path of the plane that rose above me. as i fell, in those last moments, i felt the long path of my existence.

300 million years ago, light-energy from the nearby star reaching this planet and locking up in plants as long chains of carbons, sugar and cellulose, then dying, sinking, lying under its own weight, compressing slowly into oil, being pumped out of the ground, refined into gasoline, thickened with polystyrene and benzene, filled into this tube with a white phosphorus nipple, loaded up onto the wing by boy-faced sailors their tattoos glistening in the sun, full of fuck this and fuck that, farting and high-fives, bolting me down and patting me once for luck, then shot into the air by a sub-deck piston, airborne to here, now hurtling through air and trees to impact on the forest floor next to a chicken coop and some women threshing rice by their thatched home.

the white phosphorus trigger exploded, the casing shattered and every ray of sunlight that lay inside me for 300 million years came shearing out as i shot and furied, sucking all the oxygen out of the air, insatiable, consuming anything that could burn in my path — the chicken coop with all the chickens, the rice and the women who were tossing it on their woven trays, the thatch on the homes and the children resting in them to avoid the mid-day heat, and a hundred meter swath of forest that lay beyond the huts. all these things and more.

all joining me in my luminous release

drop

dear cloud

i've been a drop in a cloud. just for you.

the dry season was ending. the seas warming off the coast. i was merged with the saltwater, drifting aimlessly along the surface of the open ocean, but got caught by a hard wind and blown off in spray from the wave-hammered surface, a microscopic bit of fluid, light enough to float. i found myself lifted skyward in ascending columns of warm wet air, up and up, higher and higher, the ocean falling away below, extending outwards to the horizon, a broad expanse of shimmering blue and grey.

The air cooled as it rose and at a certain point, when it had gotten cold enough, the moisture in it condensed.

across the sea, far off in all directions, at precisely the same elevation, rising columns of moist ocean air whitened into clouds that continued to rise in their now visible forms, billowing up above the updrafts that fed them like steam over kettles, rising higher and higher into towering sculptures of thick mist.

at first white, then darkening under their own shadows, these many separate clouds began to grow and fuse with each other, changing over many hours into a single front of black and grey a hundred miles long that slid slowly inland, moving away from the sea and over the savanna, boiling upwards as electric thunderheads, small strikes of lightning sparking cloud to cloud, growing increasing opaque, blotting out the sun from the world below.

down there were hills of red laterite, blue-green watering holes, canyons, dry riverbeds, and grasslands far off into the distance. all that fell under our shadow and darkened, their subtle patterns disappearing into an all consuming grey. and yet, even from so high above i could sense that that darkening world was alive. across the endless grassy plain, herds of blue wildebeests ran shoulder to shoulder, intermixed here and there with groups of zebra, flowing through the grass by the thousands, a tide of glistening backs. they moved and the land moved. drifting. flowing. from beneath their countless hooves, dust swelled and rose, unfurling in tan clouds that lifted toward the dark clouds above them. the dust rose on the hot dry air until it hit us and drew us in like magnets. lightning cracked. i clung to a mote of floating dust and fell as a drop of rain.

hurtling downward toward the savanna, i was shaped into a tear, stretching longer as my speed increased, heady, dizzying, falling with a million other drops at breakneck speed toward the swelling ocean of grunts and bellows and thrusting upturned horns that covered the land below us, the rumble of their hooves matching the thunder we returned.

falling closer and closer, the many backs became clearer as i neared, from thousands to hundreds, from hundreds to one, a single male wildebeest slick with sweat, its back ridged with matted bristle shuddering as he ran. i struck his blunt muzzle mixing with sweat and dust on rough hide, only to slip off, and pass briefly through the hot air huffing from his froth-edged mouth. down i fell between his running legs and caught finally on the arching tip of a blade of dropseed, clinging to it, dripping down its ragged edges. down the curl of the stalk i slipped to where a small locust gripped itself tightly to the blade, tearing with its pincered mandibles at the edges of the leaf, eating away at its world little chomp by little chomp, oblivious to the tide of flesh flowing around it. i came to rest against the locust, sliding down its side like a tiny bead of sweat on its beige and ruby shell.

on the leg of the locust, in the shadow of its pulsing belly, was a tiny red dot, just a pin prick. a mite, its eight little legs latched onto the locust like manacles. i slipped down next to it and merged. inside the mite, except for the small tremors that passed through my chitinous skin when the grasshopper chirped, and the vague sense of air moving over my back, everything else about the world fell away.

there, in a red mite, tucked under the belly of locust, on one of the billion blades of serengeti grass, amid the rumbling dust of the migrating wildebeest herd, in the shadow of a hundred miles of boiling black thunderheads, everything was as close and still as a cave. i felt i could rest there forever.

i don't know why i do these things

i'm just along for the ride

temple bell

dear cloud

i have been a bronze bell, hung in a old country temple.

at the upper end of a long mountain valley, high above terraced fields of shockgreen rice and thatched houses huddled shoulder to shoulder in the shadows of hills like sudden walls, were a set of roughhewn stone steps. just the few bottom steps could be seen from the fields, the rest disappeared steeply up into the halflight of the forest, lurching up the hillside in a desperate act of ascension. at the top, far above the valley floor, hidden among the thick trunks of ancient trees, sat a temple built on a perch of level land that looked out over the valley when the mists allowed. it was not a grand temple, no more than a single wooden hall with a bowed bark roof and a separate bell tower off to one side. tower might be too grand a word. it was just four sturdy posts holding up a shingle roof beneath which was slung a heavy beam, strong enough to carry the weight of the huge bell. the bell was the pride of all the villagers who lived along the valley. they had scrimped and saved for years to have enough to donate to the priest so he could pay for it to be cast, and when it was ready every able-bodied person, young and old, joined in the heavy work of carrying it back from a river town five days walk to the north.

i had come to this valley as a mendicant, making a pilgrimage to all the small temples in the area, barefoot, without possessions, bringing nothing more than the clothes on my back, my battered reed hat and heavy walking staff. i had merged with the monk after following him through a small village. he seemed so at ease with the world, placid face lit by a permanent halfsmile. at ease but also somehow determined, marching on as he did single-mindedly, devoid of comforts, constant in his pursuit.

i traveled from village to village, tracing the narrow tracks that passed for roads through tilled fields and orchards in blossom, across hillpasses to yet another village with its fields and orchards and so on through the country. the further i went, the steeper the paths became, irregularly used and strewn with stones, passing through tangled forests and hills choked with grass bamboo. it was a tiring journey. i kept my focus by imagining before me a clear light to which i was walking.

i would begin each day just before dawn. what a magic hour that was, the world coming to life around me in ways large and small. the water of the earth warming and rising as mist. small birds flitting from the trees. light filling all the spaces that had just been shadow. and as i walked, day after day, year after year, the forward motion of my body became its own inertia, the path felt like a stream, the weight of all the days behind me water at my back, urging me closer toward the light, toward whatever epiphany it was that awaited me, a moment of breaking through that i could just taste, that i could feel waiting around each corner, at the top of each rise. each morning as i set off on my walk my first step would bring the thought.

perhaps today.

perhaps today.

for days, for months, the feeling would build in me, the rising expectation that this forward motion, this deprivation and focus, was bringing me steadily and inescapably toward some moment of understanding. a joyous release. it was a wonderful feeling, a giddy feeling, to walk each day in a state of such bliss — a hyper-awareness of minutia and great movements all at once — dragonfly eyes and constellations, ferns and forests, all flowing through my mind as part of one comfortable thought.

but this was not to last.

it could be any day, in any place, and the feeling would

vanish. i might smell something cooking, grilling dump-
lings or whatever, wafting up from a hut, or i would catch
the sweetness of ripened persimmons in the autumn air,
and as i walked my mind would fill with strange hallucina-
tions of food — rice and wine and steaming plates of fried
vegetables — and my own gnashing teeth chewing their
way through it all.

once i saw a farmgirl working bent in a field, her skirt
tucked up into her crotch to keep it out of the mud, showing her strong tan legs. her smock hung open loosely as she
worked threshing back and forth, revealing small pointed
breasts, and my breath rose inside me as i fell into dreams
of sweaty rutting.

another time i remember crossing paths with a gang
of young toughs, strutting and shouting, kicking dogs and
children out of their way. my head dropped as i plowed on
but my mind washed bloodred, my staff cracking skulls in
spiraling fantasies of power that took many days walk to
dissipate.

so often i would lose my way. then the mist would
open and i would sit for hours, lost in the sheer beauty of
the mountains. and start again. the weight of the walking
pushing me forward. and upward.

i remember little of how i got to the valley, the exact
particulars of the road, the day or the weather. i remember
only silently greeting villagers who had come out of their
homes to put small alms in my bowl, and then climbing the

long flight of steps up through the scattered light dappling the grass bamboo that grew thickly on the forest floor. when i reached the top of the stairs, i leaned against a tree to catch my breath just as a young monk came out of the temple hall and walked over to the bell tower. i followed him as he climbed up onto the platform by the bell, and stood below watching as he prepared to strike, pulling back on the heavy palm-trunk ram that hung there for that purpose. realizing what he was about to do, i placed my palms together by my breast in reverence and bowed my head just as the ram came swinging back and struck the metal.

the sound was pure. absolute. flowing through me and within me and out across the valley. it contained within it immensities. it was the forest and the light, the constellations and streams, the wings of the moth and the unmoving mountain. all this was caught within its timbre and tone as if the world were just vibrations and this bell the voice that gave them form.

i flowed up within the bell merging with it and rang and rang and rang. even when still, i could feel that sound within me just waiting to be released.

i had walked so far in hopes of being struck

what do you want from me

dear cloud

i have been a long distance traveler for 10,000 years. give or take. i know you really want data about this planet — very specific data — calibrations and quantifications; detailed research to add to the great body of knowledge that makes you what you are, cloud of knowledge celestial, eternal and all-seeing. *and here i give you random thoughts and ramblings. does it bore you. in the beginning i thought you might give up on me. now i know you won't. but neither do you answer. i open to you and speak my mind, and all i get is silence. an emptiness so vast it doesn't even echo.*

hello?
        hello?

why do i need to know you're there. i'm so happy just being.

111

baobob

dear cloud

i have been a baobab tree on a dry plain.

when i first merged with the tree, i was growing alone
among scrub brush and grass. the tallest thing around for
miles. i had been there for so long, even the rivers changed
their courses while i grew. when i was young, my trunk was
thick, straight and smooth, a silvergrey that held moonlight
even in the day. giraffe would stand in my shade to get out
of the hot sun and rub their long necks on my bark. at
night, bats would gather to my flowers, which hung upside
down on long vines like bangles. white, full, inverted explo-
sions of petals and stamens.

now i've thickened and wizened into a hoary thing, big

as a house, with withered folds and hollows in my skin. in recent years, people came and settled next to me, building themselves a small village. they made simple pole lean-tos around my trunk, and gather in them each day for their market. the ground in a wide circle all around me is bare of grass and packed by the passing of many feet.

they come to barter. they come to dance and sing.

if some raise their voices in argument others speak in whispers. it all comes into me and resides in my wet cork flesh.

at first it was the giraffe and other wild things. now the people gather within the circle of my outstretched branches.

> i am the tall friend with long arms
> and shelter all who come to me

dear cloud

i have been a baker of bread.

in a small village in the mountains that clung to the steep slopes above the river, perched between the pastures below and the forests further up, in a small stone building that snuggled shoulder to shoulder with all the other buildings along the main street, i ran a bakery. the heavy wooden sign that hung out front had a carving showing a sheath of wheat bound in the middle and splayed.

my mother had been the village baker before me, and her mother before her.

it was said that every person in the village came

through the bakery at least once a week. there was only one bakery and bread is, as they say, the staff of life. as the people came through so came their stories. where some towns had newspapers, in our small village we had my bakery and what wasn't spoken within the walls of my shop wasn't worth knowing. births and deaths, success and failures, passion and pain. it filled the air of my small shop as surely as the scent of baked bread.

each morning well before dawn i would rise to begin the day's work. walking down the stairs from my second-floor rooms into the dark kitchen, still warm from the day before, i would take a bundle of twigs from the brush pile and relight the fire in the oven, adding increasingly large pieces of wood until a warm glow came from the open oven doors. from a cupboard nearby, i would take a large ceramic bowl covered with a wet cloth that held the poolish, which had been warming all night in the leftover heat from the old brick oven. it would be filled with bubbles and smell sour and warm. adding flour to make the right consistency for dough, i would tip it out on the counter to begin the long process of kneading and forming the loaves.

i always kept the poolish in the back of the shop, in a cupboard next to the warm oven, not only to rise, but so as to be away from all the gossiping that went on in the front. this is the way my mother taught me and the way she heard it from her mother before her. wet poolish she said is a sponge, impressionable, and must be kept away from all *that*, nodding her scarfed head toward the front of the shop where the vagaries of the world were spoken.

when i began each morning, the poolish would be clean, pure. with added flour it became a pad to write my thoughts on. as i bent to the kneading, i would think back on the good things i had heard the day before. only the good things. the dough would stretch and fold, and on each push and turn i would bring to mind some point of joy or light. this was as my mother had taught.

the dough stretched out on the old wooden counter like some ancient living book, open and ready to be scribed, and i brought to mind the woman from the green house at the end of town whose son had just come back from years at sea, how all the endless days of waiting and terrible thoughts of calamities, wild storm-tossed oceans and violent shipwrecks, that had lived within her mind unspoken, creasing her once-pretty face, how all those thoughts had fallen from her and how she walked easily and spoke with an excited speed that even she could not keep up with, her words catching on each other as they tumbled out. i thought about her and folded that into the still wet dough. once. turn. twice. turn. then again.

there was the just-married couple who still walked about as if in one body, magnetic to each other, their eyes constantly rolling to glance at the miracle that was their own company. they would speak at the same time, giggle at themselves and start again. they fed each other small bits of pastries, watching closely how each other's lips moved, awed and grateful that anything so wonderful should have been born into this world. i would think about their youthful blushes and fold that inside. once. turn. twice. turn. again.

an old man smoking his pipe, who sat in the window of the bakery at the small table we kept there for people who had time to linger, who would listen to anyone's troubles if they cared to talk and who had for each worried person the same words of comfort. that too shall pass. that too shall pass. i would think about his clean-shaven face, soft and open, and fold that within. once. turn. twice. turn. then again.

and there were my own thoughts. the flowers in all the blue boxes that the villagers hung from their windowsills, blossoming red and white and red and white down through every street and alley.

herds of sheep in our green pastures as the sun closed toward the mountaintops and all the world was lit with a horizontal light that gave form and dimension to even the smallest thing, making the sheep look like balls of cotton dotting the smooth meadows.

the sound of the stony river falling quickly near the old bridge, where on a starlit evening many years ago, pressed against the heavy wooden rails i got my first kiss. a burbling rushing sound that, once heard, i found had stayed within me, quickening in the hollow of my chest with its memory.

these too i would fold within the elastic dough and they would rise into loaves by the warmth of the old brick oven and return into the world as fresh-baked bread.

there are many ways   i have found
    to return the blessings we encounter

hollow

dear cloud

i have been a hollow, carved by water into stone.

at first, i was a raccoon cub. it was spring. the whole gaze was frolicking together along the banks of a quick stream. gnawing at driftwood. sniffing under fallen logs. pawing over pebbles to look for grubs. there was a peach-colored pebble, round as a marble, and when i flipped it to look underneath, it pittered a little ways down the slope toward the stream. i hopped over to it and pawed it again. again it rolled. pittery pattery stop. i hopped. pawed. it rolled. again and again all the way down to the stream where, with one last push, i sent it tumbling off a drop into the quick-moving water. when it fell in, i merged with it and plop, in too i went.

the snowmelt from the mountains was strong and the force of the cold water sent me tumbling along the stream bottom through strands of bent grasses out into the middle where the current took me between huge boulders too heavy to roll, through the tongues of whitewater that shot out from them in long vees, knocking across the bony rapids, straight past backwashes that pulled at me to no avail, through flashes of bright sunlight that sparkled in the sandpocked water, through deep shadows below the overhanging branches of pines, on and on downstream spinning in dizzy rotations, until, with a dull muted thunk, i dropped into a small hollow in the bottom of the stream, perfectly round, about two feet deep.

the way the stream flowed over the hollow, curved into a liquid bow, it sent the water in the hollow spinning around in a circle. i found myself rattling around at the bottom of the hollow with ten or so other stones of varying sizes, caught in this riparian centrifuge, joined unwittingly to a team of little grindstones eating away at the walls of our host. for several weeks i stayed in there, clinking around in restless perambulations, a dizzy pilgrim circumscribing a newfound holyland, but when the ice jams upstream finally succumbed to the inevitable urges of the season, breaking up under the weight of the sun, the flood waters came barreling down the streambed with such sudden intensity that they washed out all the stones from the hollow in one fell swoop. when they went, i stayed behind in the hard wall i had been carving.

once the sculptor, now the sculpted.

the floodwaters subsided and a new crew of grinders took the place of the last, rattling around inside me, giving of themselves peck by peck to make me bigger. i grew thanks to their mindless churning. but not they. all who leave me leave smaller. the sum total of what they've lost in shed skin would be my exact volume.

i began, it would seem, from a tiny imperfection in the crystalline structure of the quartzite riverbed. a pebble hit that spot by chance, and then another and another. the resulting chip in time became a cleft, then a depression, then a bowl, then a kettle. the pebbles that fell in me to stay a day a month or a year, did their work unerringly, orbiting my inner ocean. because i was softer than they, they widened me and deepened me.

in the end   i am what i am
        because of my weakness

homeward bound

dear cloud

i have been a man homeward bound.

i saw him lying on the edge of a field filled with pale
autumn grasses and sunshine, where countless humming
insects whirred in small circles around themselves, each a
spiraling mote of honeylight. blue flowers dotted through
the grasses, gathering in the hollows of the field like pools
of water. the man was lying very still, his back resting on
an old stone wall that was crumbling in places and pocked
with weeds. above him spread an ancient tree, huge, gnarled
and knotted, its thick branches heavy with golden leaves.
the sun lit the wall where he rested and although the air had
the chill of winter-coming, it looked warm where he was,

such a nice place to rest, in the shelter of the wall, beneath the outspread arms of the tree, by the quietly autumnal meadow bathed in angled light. he slouched, holding his belly, back propped up against the wall, chin on his chest. i thought he was sleeping. how wrong could i have been. i merged and awoke into a sea of pain.

a man knows when he's going to die. it's not a smell but it's like a smell, or some ancient bone-cloak that rattles in to clothe him for his journey. i could not breathe for the pain. it was all i could do to grit my teeth and suck weak hisses of air, eyes pressed shut.

shit shit shit, i moaned. i let a long breath out, took one back in, silently mouthed the name of my son across split and quivering lips. two more days walk, just two maybe three and you'd be home, you idiot. how could you let this happen.

i cracked my eyelids just enough to see where my hands lay cupped on my belly, lifting them just a little. they felt wet and sticky. and heavy, so impossibly heavy. the fingers stuck together with drying blood. beneath them a stain soaked through my tattered uniform like a widening shadow. i pulled my shirt opened as softly as i could. the edges of the wound were encrusted with a yellow-grey powder, the center black.

a thick leather cartridge belt lay slung across my waist. below that, my legs shot out in odd directions. laces worn out, my tattered boots lay open like flayed animals, covered with the scars of too many miles. beyond my feet the meadow swam around, a huge nebulous gulf of dizzy ochre waves rolling and shifting sickeningly. eyes rheumy with age and powder burns, all the bright spots in the meadow burst and blurred into hot coronas. the shadows fell away, deep and vague. indiscernible. all those spinning motes of light that had drawn me in at first appeared now not as insects but as lit vortexes spiraling up and cast into my brain, circling and carrying me with them into nausea.

as i watched, lightheaded, the ochre light in the meadow became the dappled pattern of leafshadows on a clay wall. i could see my son walking past the wall, slowly, in a dark hat, walking ever so slowly as if through water, bobbing along in front of the wall, his head rolling leisurely with his steps, then turning in the awareness of being watched. slowly, his head turned until he faced me where i sat, across the square outside the old café. he watched me while he walked in the leaflight along the wall, looking over his shoulder at me, eyes glinting like obsidian, a gentle blush casting over his face. a knowing smile rose from the corners of his wide mouth when he saw me and he burst in a surge of light that became the all-too-bright meadow. i closed my eyes and rested.

i tried opening my eyes again but the sunlight erupted as a slow powder flash at the base of my brain. a boy's face jumped out of the light, turned and sank away. i closed my eyes but felt dizzy that way. when i opened them to stop the nausea, there was that boy's face again rising out of the light, open-mouthed, eyes wide, momentarily there and then gone. opening and closing my eyes like that, i slipped in and out of light and dark until i passed out.

when i came to my tongue was dry and fat, a cow's tongue too big for my own mouth. *water*, i croaked and then thought, ahh shit. if anyone heard.

it was the war, of course. i had been away fighting for 21 maybe 22 months by then. well, nearly two years in any case. we all hated it. if we weren't bored to death we were scared shitless. that's all there was. day in day out. and for the life of me, i had no idea what we were doing there. no one did. oh sure. kill the red-hats, that much we all knew. but no one really remembered what the whole thing was about.

march there, hold this line. take that hill. burn this village. move back across the valley. as time went by, no one could seem to recollect the plan, if ever there was one, and we lived increasingly for small things — a hot meal, a little clean water, a cigarette. that's all that really mattered. the days stretched out pointlessly, no end in sight, and we just slogged through it, stunned, our thoughts empty of any hope or purpose.

last night.... was it last night. was it two days ago, my god i can't remember. well anyway, it was night, that much i know, and we got caught in crossfire. cannon and rifles un-loading across us in both directions all night. i kept down, my face pressed against a ragged bedroll that smelled of old sweat, hunkered into some scraggy bushes, shivering, feeling so small and scared. all night, the barrages contin-ued, everyone groveling into whatever crack or crevice they could find and all night we lay shaking and crying, muffled whimpering and whispered prayers coming from every bush and stony hollow. i mouthed the name of my son over and over. his mother died giving birth to him and he was all i had. i repeated his name as a prayer, as if the enunciation alone would somehow draw him to me. pull him over the hills to me. or me to him.

exhausted to the point of not caring, eventually i slept and when i woke it was to an eerie quiet. a mist ran low through the valley and there was not a sound to be heard. it was so strange. this is not good, i thought, not good at all. no cannon. no birds. nothing stirring. i figured i'd been killed and thought, so this is what's it's like.

but my hands moved in front of me. my rifle felt like it always felt. my bedroll still smelled like shit.

i lay there just listening for sounds for the longest time and when it seemed i *was* alive and quite alone, i wriggled out of the bush and stood to look around. i turned in a slow circle, taking in everything — the trees torn by can-nonfire, branches hanging limp and broken, the river at the bottom of the meadow, mist rising from it, the old stone bridge across the river choked on both sides with the corpses of soldiers, the hills off in the distance, and in all that, nothing moved and no one spoke. and that's when it struck me. i had come this far. i wasn't dead. and, neither had i killed. a miracle. my slate was still clean. i kept looking at the hills, gazing at them trying to make them out with my tired eyes, thinking about where i lived somewhere beyond them. i was thinking about home, about my village and my son, and it was some time before i realized i was already walking. i kept expecting someone to yell at me to come back. or to shoot at me. but that never happened and i just kept walking toward the distant hills. it was all so strange. so peaceful and so unreal. i was homeward bound.

the sun came up, warm, even though the autumn air was crisp. it was lovely. i waded through fields of wheat like hip-deep water, passed an orchard, ate a few apples, and then came to a long view over the fields across a valley to the hills i needed to cross. the warm light was falling softly over everything. it was all beautiful and unreal. how, just *how* could the world still hold this for me.

as i walked, i thought of my son playing with his friends in the village square. i remembered sitting outside the café, passing time reading the paper and watching the children play in the dappled light under the trees by the old wall of the church. he was walking with some of the other boys along the wall and turned to look at me, smiling with his mother's black black eyes. my dreams drew me closer to him. and him to me.

i walked all morning until i came to a wide field filled with flowers. across the field was an old stone wall and a huge tree covered in golden leaves. it was so beautiful. the tree. the meadow so quiet, filled with flowers and whirring insects. no one around for miles. i walked up to the tree and stopped to look up at it, its thick black branches spreading out in all directions into its cloak of leaves. i wiped my forehead, looked out over the hills in the distance i still had to cross and took a step toward the wall.

just as i took that step, a boy with a long gun popped up from where he had been hiding behind the wall. he looked so scared, mouth hanging opened, eyes shock wide, his gun pointed flat at my gut and we stood there for a strangely poised moment just looking at each other like we knew one another. then he shot. i felt a sound too loud to be heard, as fire and smoke spat from the muzzle of his gun. the slug passed right though me, low down by my belt. the pain knocked the breath out of me and we hung there, he and i, both stunned at the sight of each other, staring wide-eyed, mouths agape. then, reflexively, i swung my gun up and shot back. the bullet went straight through his neck. he made one short gurgling cough and his eyes went quiet. they were very dark, his eyes, and they just went so quiet and dull, like wet pebbles drying. he turned, took one step, and fell.

laying by the wall, i remembered walking away from the war, getting shot, shooting back. a sickness welled up inside me at the memory and i vomited blood on my own chest, coughing weakly for a while and then slumping into a grey stupor. when i came to again the sun was getting low. i tried to remember the boy's face but it was all so confusing. everything was getting dark and cold. i kept thinking about my own son instead. i imagined myself walking across the field, the warm sunlight, the old tree, the stone wall, and the boy popping up, but in my mind it was now *my* boy, *my* son who had jumped out from behind the wall.

wait. what's going on, i thought. that wasn't my son. i couldn't be home yet. how far did i walk. how far could i have walked anyway. could he have been coming to find me.

no. that boy was older than my son. but wait. of course, two years have gone by. i've been away for two years. could my boy have grown that much.

wait. wait. wait. that tree. i know that tree. the wall and that tree. no. it's not possible. how far did i walk anyway.

i remembered again walking up to the stone wall and the boy popping up from the other side. his face was clear this time. i could see his face. i knew his face and, in a hoarse voice, i called the name of my son.

no. it couldn't be. i shot my boy?

you crazy blind old fuck. you shot your boy.

i had to see. i had to know. calling his name, i pushed myself up slowly. my legs were useless so i rolled over and dragged myself up the wall, trailing blood up and over the grey stones. sliding down the other side i saw the boy lying face down on the ground. the back of his neck was all blown out and bloody. i crawled over to him and pushed him with shaking hands to turn him over. his head lolled around on his broken neck — his eyes were still open. he had dark black eyes. obsidian eyes. just like my son. i called his name.

> eyes like my son
>> but not my son.
>>> not my son.

i reached out to close his eyes my hand sweeping across his face, wiping away the dirt on his cheek. as if that would help. as if that would make it all better. i pushed his hair back and then slumped, racked with coughing, took a few deep breaths to calm down, and dragged myself up so my face was right next to his, this boy with obsidian eyes. i called him by son's name and kissed him once on lips still barely warm, then laid my head on his chest to sleep.

i stayed by that wall for a long time. long after the villagers came to look for the boy and carried him home on their shoulders, filling the fields with their wailing. long after they returned and hacked at my body with shovels and scythes, after they strung me up by one foot from that ancient tree so i hung torn and splayed like some foully dressed game. long after the local boys came back for target practice with their old hunting guns, hooting and howling and slapping each other on the back with each hit. long after my body blackened and rotted and fell to pieces save a single booted foot left dangling from that old tree like an unfinished thought.

i stayed there by the crumbling wall, in the weeds and the stones, and the rolling meadow turning white into winter, and thought on this for a long, long time.

tumbling

dear cloud

i have knocked around this world now for so many years, a tumbleweed in the wind, a leaf caught in the currents of a wide river, slipping along at the will of the water. and what i bump against, i become… pond to pine to moss to man.

it's all serendipity and happenstance. something appears in my path and i become it. and then something else. and then another. and another.

through all this, the shifting forms and bodies, the many points of view large and small, still and moving, i feel a pattern revealing itself. a pattern but not a purpose.

i see clearly the fabric but not the reason for the cloth.

perhaps you know? i wonder.

crossroads

dear cloud

i have been a woman at a crossroads.

i was driving my chevy to the melody motel to meet a new friend. the car glided through the flat landscape like a stone across ice. smooth. real, real smooth. i took a sip of the highball and put the sweat-beaded glass back in the holder. tammy wynette was standing by her man on the radio and i was waiting to match her on the refrain. i'm not bad, you know, not bad when i get going. each time the part came around, i'd take a sip of the jack n' coke, pull a long drag off my slimladymenthol and puff clouds of sadness into the rear view mirror. i caught myself reflected there, raccoon eyes ultra-lashed, a bouffant like wind-blown cotton candy, and reached up to sweep a few loose strands back up into the pile of big hair. i blew another cloud of smoke out the side of my mouth and changed my mind, pulling down a few strands, twisting them around my finger and letting them hang in a curl down my cheek. loose. just a little loose.

i tapped off the ash from my cig with the tips of my long fingers and noticed that the patch of bloodred lipstick on the filter matched my maybelline nails.

it was nice like this, driving cross-country on a late afternoon, real nice, the car slipping over the asphalt like air, the summer sun sinking low over my shoulder, those highballs rounding the edges off everything. even the stony tumbleweed land stretching unbroken to the horizon seemed somehow filled with light, softened and rounded. this was going to be alright.

the half-busted airconditioner fan ticked away, struggling to keep the summer heat out of the car. as the sun settled further down in the west, angling in the driver-side window like a huge arc light, my blouse began to stick to the vinyl seat and i leaned forward, tugging at the back of it to let some air in. feeling the strap of my bra cutting, i reached back and tugged at it once to loosen things. i thought of how i looked that morning after showering and doing my hair, seeing myself in the dresser mirror, my maidenform tits like taut white pyramids, sitting proud and high against deeply tanned skin. i turned to see them from all angles propping them up with my hands, grabbing my butt and giving it a good squeeze. not bad. not great but not half bad if you know what i mean. then i slipped on a pressed-white blouse, just a little see-through, and left a couple buttons opened. just a little loose.

i knew he'd have trouble with my top. with those thick, calloused fingers he'd fumble with the little buttons. that's ok i thought. i'll undo them for him. he'll just stand there watching me. my breath got short just thinking about it, butterflies, and i liked that. i thought how he'd stare as i slowly revealed my collarbones, my belly button, the line of peach fuzz that leads down from there into my panties. i saw myself reaching back to unclip the bra, slip it slowly from my shoulders, nipples hard in the cool motel air.

i bit my lip and laughed to myself, took a deep pull on the slimlady and blew out the smoke long and slow. my thighs pressed together to push the feeling down and the engine revved. one more puff and a sip of the highball to calm down. nice. real nice. i nodded my head and glanced around at the dry land, wincing at the bright sun hanging low out my side window.

earlier that day, i had been sitting outside my trailer thinking about what to say if he called. would he ask me to meet him at the melody like he'd said he would. would i go if he did. i thought about it long and hard, sitting there drink in hand on the front steps under a tattered beach umbrella i had wired to the handrail. i sat there looking at that road that just went out and on forever, thining how nothing good ever came down it and how nothing ever would. i thought about meeting this guy at the state fair, how good he looked, cleancut hairs above his white collar, a cleft in his well-shaved chin, his strong back. strong hands. working hands. a plain gold ring on one finger.

i thought about my life stretching on as long and thin and dry as that road, and when the phone rang i was driving before i answered.

the sun kept sinking lower, almost to the horizon, a fiery orb settling on a land that dried and scalded beneath it. i tried to swivel the visor over to block the light but the damn thing pulled off in my hand, so i chucked it in the back seat. the left side of my face glowed, like sitting next to an open furnace. i rested my left hand on my temple to block the sunlight and looked out ahead. ten more miles, give or take. i glanced at the clock on the dash but it was stuck at some time in the past.

i took another sip of the highball, draining it, rattling the remnants of the ice cubes around a bit, then lit another menthol.

the sign at the next crossroads read plainville 5 with an arrow pointing right, and paradise 20 pointing left to the sun. it didn't say what was up ahead or how far it was but that's where i was going. i pressed the pedal down and cruised into the crossing.

everything that happened after that, happened so slowly. at least that's the way i remember it now. i was pulling a long drag on my menthol and about to give a shoutout to tammy, when a huge shadow crossed the sun and the fiery spotlight outside snapped off. i turned to see what it was but nothing could have prepared me for what was there. a huge sacrificial altar, glorious and exultant, a vast chromium grillework sat upon by a wild-eyed silver dog had been born from the sun and was right there outside my window only a few feet away, hurtling toward me at enormous speed. caught in rapture at the sight, a great halo of light bursting out from behind the altar, i noticed that behind the silver-dog, high up above it in an enclosed podium, sat an angel in white. white t-shirt. white cowboy hat. a chubby, boy-faced angel, his eyes insanely wide in disbelief.

are you so surprised to see me, i thought as the angel and his dog bore down on me.

all the windows in the car suddenly exploded into millions of tiny shards, crystallizing white and then vanishing as if sucked away. the wind was in the car and my hair blew wild and loose, the sleeves tearing off my shirt in complete abandon.

the word tornado flew through my head.

everything began drifting sideways in front of my eyes — the road, the sign posts, the endless flat landscape.

a thunderclap exploded in my ears so sudden and loud that it pushed out tornado and every other word i had ever known, leaving a blank slab of dull stone on which to record my revelation.

the side of my car flashed with sparks and buckled in, shoving me toward the middle of the seat as we skidded together, the altar and i, screeching across the pavement and off the road.

the next thing i remember, i was pulling my head up from the dashboard and the world had stopped moving. i sat frozen for a long time, a hundred years if it was a minute. the thunderclap still echoed in my ears like an ocean in a shell. there were things in front of my eyes, colors and out of focus shapes, but no particular meaning to any of them. a white squarish thing. a beige one, long and flat. a blue field above it all. a dot of red. slowly, the bleary shapes sharpened into forms and some words appeared on the stone in my brain.

sun

the sun was there again, in front of me now, resplendent, wrapped within a vast corona of red light, hovering just at the horizon.

truck

an 18-wheeler sat not far away buckled and askew, its cab plowed into a grass bank at the edge of the road.

melody

what on earth could that mean.

woman

in the rear view mirror there sat a woman with wild hair, the left half of her face studded with hundreds of small diamonds and painted in long trails of dripping liquid the exact shade of her lipstick. a burnt out cigarette hung from her stunned lips. her raccoon eyes were smeared and filled with tears.

angel

the angel was walking around the truck, flapping his arms, trying to fly.

i sat at that crossroads for what seemed like forever, in a time outside of time, no longer fully within my body and not completely out. i watched as the ignited orb of the sun widened and sank below the horizon. i felt the wind come hot and dry though the windowless car. the sign for paradise pointed straight ahead now.

maybe good things do happen to me on this road.

there are crossroads where you chose
and crossroads where you're chosen

bamboo

dear cloud

i have been a forest of bamboo, a hundred acres of straight green culms marked at intervals by sharp rings, some erect, some leaning, some dead and fallen, caught and hung across the others, the overlapping lines slicing the views within me into a thousand pieces.

on a windless day, the air inside me was as still as a held breath. few plants grew there so deep was my shade, so jealous my thirst for whatever rainwater fell to the ground, and with few plants, neither were there many animals living within me. when the wind was still, you could hear my new shoots stretching out of the ground, easing aside the deep layers of fallen leaves that had built up within me, shoots like fat pointed pistons expanding imperceptibly but steadily toward the leafy canopy above them.

in the slightest breeze, my many stems would sway softly from side to side, the ones that lay across each other, touching and creaking as they rubbed, giving off a haunting sound like the mating call of some long extinct bird, clear yet coming from nowhere in particular, at once earthly and ethereal. what a strange place i was on those days, the sunlight passing intermittently through openings in the leaf cover, cutting down through the dark air, bleeding galaxies of soft-dappled light onto the ground that washed back and forth as if caught in surf.

and when the wind blew hard, i blew with it, my leafy heads tossing as wildly as the long hair of a shamaness, ecstatic, undulating for the pleasure of the gods. bending madly with the wind then snapping back against it, surging back and forth, shedding old leaves and small twigs by the ton but never coming close to breaking.

i was a place in two parts — the wild reaches on the steep slopes of the mountains, and the tended groves near the village. in the mountains i was a tangle of every trunk that had grown, leaned or fallen, a jumble of green and brown poles so thick and interwoven that even the deer walked around me. near the village, however, i was cleaned of all debris. the people there dug and leveled the land into terraces, swept the fallen leaves into neat rows that surrounded each level pad. they collected the new shoots to eat, felled the thicker culms to use for fences and walls and the lighter stems for making fine utensils. i was brighter there, more airy and open.

the children would throw small rocks into me, hurling them with all their strength at the thousands of tall stems receding into the distance. those pebbles would hit one stem and bounce to another, then another and another. they would count the thunks out loud, their faces lighting as the numbers increased. i counted with them. it was a good game.

the wind in my leaves, the green stems, the dappled light, all beautiful and yet i was strongest where out of sight. my gnarly roots spread out from each tree, a knotted explosion of snaking wood. from nodes along those roots new shoots would spring up and grow, and from those shoots another blast of fibrous roots would radiate outward, and so on and so on until the entire mountainside, in one huge sweep up from the village to the heights where points of granite lay exposed and worn, the ground was a single interwoven mat of roots. if you were to lift me up with some huge hand, i'm sure i would tear off the hill in one piece in a grizzled mat.

tomorrow, the villagers will come to chop me down. one part of me, that is. it's not hard to do. though my stems may look sturdy, they are thin-walled and hollow. a saw will make quick work of it. even a heavy blade at just the right angle with just the right speed will slice clear through me. i am hollow so i cut easily. i am hollow so i split into strips that the villagers find useful for their tool-making. i am hollow so i grow quickly. i am hollow so i bend before the gale.

> if i am anything
>> it is because at my very core
>>> i am utterly empty

millboy

dear cloud

i have been a young man in a place of many sounds.

i would come to them each day and they would fill me and awaken me, and i would live within them and because of them.

it was an old brick factory in a seaside town, a salty squat box hunkered down by the bay, just one among others large and small, all crowded up around the ends of long wooden docks that stuck akilter into the dark waters. each was surrounded by a high brick wall and each had its own smokestack jutting up into the slate sky. anyday but sunday, lazy coalsmoke streams would be found drifting leeward from them, shading the air with a pall of fine dust that settled on anything not moving so that the flat tops of every still thing in the city were coated black: walls, lamp-posts, stacks of empty boxes in the alleys. the grit settled on the ledges of the small-paned windows and ran in dark tearstains down the walls.

i had been a rat, scampering along the top of a wall near the crowd of workers as they shuffled through the iron gate into the factory one morning early, watching their tired, smudge-streaked faces. quiet. resigned. most were millgirls, young, small fingers cold, poking through mitts, hardly ready to thread and bob the mill's machines. a few were older women, matrons who oversaw the millgirls and among the dull figures there was one young man, a boy really, shy to the point of paralysis near the girls. he lingered at the back of the crowd, his long face half-hidden by a large floppy hat and a curl of jet-black hair that twisted out from beneath the brim across his forehead like a loose thought. the way he drifted along in the crowd, he was like any one of the small things that float in the bay, caught by the tide. flowing in. flowing out. rudderless. i merged with him as he passed beneath the iron gates and walked into the entrance of the factory, stumbling along after the millgirls.

inside, the sound of the steam engine greeted us, a slow steady whump whump whump punctuated by the wheez-ing and spew of the boiler. whump whump hisssss spittt whump whump hisssss. the low thumping reverberated through the building. you could feel it in your legs the way a bareback rider feels the heartbeat of their horse. whump whump whump all through the place.

   still half asleep i walked slowly a safe distance behind the crowd of girls across the lobby to the stairs and up to the next floor, padding up stone steps now cupped and rounded from the passing of many feet. the girls took up their positions at the machines and i walked over to my spot in the corner by the belt levers. from there, wide leather belts rose to drive shafts hanging from the ceiling, from which stretched more leather belts, looping across the long ceiling and down to the looms like racks of brown suspenders.

   a low whistle blew, deep and long like a foghorn, then three sharp high tweets, spaced a second apart. when i heard the third whistle, i leaned into the long lever that engaged the main belt allowing all the other drive belts to tap power off the main shaft. as the belts skidded into motion and all the looms engaged and built up speed, an animated clatter arose from the moving parts, some high-pitched, like the tickety tickety tickety of the small bobbin feeds, quick and light. some slower and heavier, like the thunk-stop thunk-stop of the shuttle arms. these and dozens more built up in overlapping rhythms, voices in a crowded room.

   day after day i lived with those sounds — the heart-thumping of the engine, the wheezy breath of the boil-er, the nervous chattering of all the hundreds of small machine parts — and over time, they became a part of me. i would hear them long after i left work, and awake only after hearing them again at the beginning of each day. i was incomplete without them.

today, after the three whistles, i engaged the belts and stayed there leaning into the heavy lever, my eyes closed, feeling the whump whump whump come up through the metal shaft, allowing it to overtake me, a child in the womb again — the warmth, the darkness, the heart beat drumming out the firmament of my universe.

something called.

i opened my eyes. on the other side of the large open room, across rows of looms with their restless armatures rising and falling in clattering waves, i saw the face of a young millgirl, pale as paper, her hair pulled back with a band into a large bun, except for some loose strands that had escaped and ran in dizzy whirlettes down the side of her face. her eyebrows were two insistent charcoal smudges, her eyes shock-blue. she was working a loom by a window that cast a hazy light filtered through its soot-streaked glass. it was as if i watched her through a tunnel, the armatures of the looms and the belts crisscrossing to make a moving jittering frame through which i could peek. i felt the pattering of the machines in my chest, a tapping like loose gears shivering in my lungs. she was looking down at her work, her hands flitting around quickly over the pulsing threads. i could feel the whump whump whumping in my chest, the bobbins clickety clicking along the edges of my bones.

the millgirls always seemed bored or tired. expressionless at their work. but this girl's face was different. her thoughts flickered across it the way sunlight ripples across the ground under trees on a windy day. appearing and disappearing, darkening and arising again. one eyebrow would lift and a smile begin, then stop and her face would go suddenly blank. then just the corner of her mouth would tighten and her eyes narrow, the passage of whatever thoughts that were bubbling within her showing up ever so slightly on her skin the way the smooth surface of a stream changes as it passes over hidden rocks.

then, in the strange unspoken way that people have of knowing they are being watched, she glanced up at me quickly, flashing her eyes across the chattering machines. in the time that we stared at each other — was it a second or two. was it more — in all that time, there was suddenly no sound.

or no. there was *only* sound. there was no me.

the heavy and soft beats, the fluttering and chattering not coming from the looms or the belts, but from everywhere at once. from the walls and the windows, from the air and the taut surface of my skin.

she looked away, quickly down at her work, and then back up at me.

the lights turning in her mind could be seen in the

small narrowings and widenings of her eyes, in a blush that warmed and flickered over her white cheeks, in the small bird-like turnings of her head, to me, away from me, to me.

we both reached up in unison to brush the curls of hair from our faces, and in unison the curls fell back down. we swept them back up but they dropped again, and at this comical pairing, the girl's nose crinkled. i tried to push the lock of hair up again but there was a wind in the place and in me and nothing would stay where it belonged, the sounds lifting off the machines and whirling up, unshackled and free, spinning through the air like promises.

for so many years the machines filled me and awakened me with their sounds and, in return, i set them free.

and all this
in an instant

enough

dear cloud

enough is enough.

i have been a long distance traveler for thousands of years. i have known life here to its fullest, been so many things for such a long time. what more could i see or hear or taste. what scents have i missed.... what feelings.   what else could i be.   oh yes. i know. the possibilities are endless. of course. i've only scratched the surface of what this world has to offer and yet...   and yet, i weary.

is there no release

when will you call me home

7316986R0

Made in the USA
Charleston, SC
17 February 2011